REAL RELATIONSHIP:

Essential Tools to Help You Go the Distance

Belden Johnson

Marriage & Family Therapist

With a Forward by Dr. Stephen Khamsi

ISBN: 1461057825
ISBN-13: 9781461057826

Dedication

To my children

Disclaimer

In this book I often give real-life examples from the lives of real people. To protect their privacy I have changed their names and disguised their circumstances, with the exception of myself and my partners, about whom I am embarrassingly frank.

Acknowledgements

If I have been able to have a bit of insight into human relationship it is primarily thanks to the fact that I have been able to stand on the shoulders of giants, from Sigmund Freud and Carl Rogers to Harville Hendrix and Marshall Rosenberg. More immediately, I have benefitted enormously from the wisdom of the women in my life, especially Yashi, Gail, Mei-yu, Nancy, Anna, and Diane. For invaluable help in clarifying my thinking about this book, I wish to thank Dr. Yashi Johnson, Dr. Stephen Khamsi, Nathanael Johnson, and Clay Jensen.
Cover image of Pablo Picasso's "The Lovers" courtesy of the National Gallery, Washington, D.C.

The minute I heard my first love story
I started looking for you, not knowing
how blind that was.

Lovers don't finally meet somewhere.
They're in each other all along.

–Jalaluddin Rumi
(1207-1273)

Translated by Coleman Barks

Foreword

I've known Belden Johnson during all three decades of my professional life. He's a big and gentle man; a family man, a father and a friend; an outstanding writer, teacher, and psychotherapist; a warm person with big ideas, a big heart and a hearty laugh. Belden works well with feelings–his own feelings, as well as those of his clients and others.

We've all got work to do on ourselves, and just about everyone has trouble with their most intimate relationships. This is, in a sense, "normal." Psychologically speaking, it's as if many individuals and couples waste their lives as they rearrange the deck chairs on the Titanic. Given this, *Real Relationship* is an important book if you're in a relationship, or if you want one. It's a guidebook for persons and for lovers that's meant to be read, to be re-read, and then to be lived. It is, in short, a game-changer. Why? Because deep feeling is the secret to real love and lasting relationships.

There are many outstanding books about relationships. But while many in our culture are happily listening to Prozac, this book describes and explains our deepest feelings and how to process them. There's a level of primal needs and feelings where much of the action takes place–both inside of individuals and between lovers. What's different here? The authenticity afforded by this book results in a depth of empathic love like no other.

Real Relationship is about many things. It's a wise book, because it understands that there is a great mystery of life, that life is about growth, and that relationships can accelerate our growth. It's a valuable book because it describes new possibilities for being real and creating intimacy in one's most intimate relationships. It's a supportive book, because it encourages us to be more authentic and emotionally honest than the culture generally allows. It's a challenging book because it asks readers to dig deep in order to experience the full range of emotions–to weep, to grieve, to shout. It's an ethical book, because it offers instruction in how to accept real responsibility and take right actions. *Real Relationship* provides clear instructions about how to strengthen personal and interpersonal integrity ... and how to make right choices in the most difficult and demanding of interpersonal situations.

You'll find wisdom in this book, both old and new. Few of us were raised with unconditional love, for example, and few of us have learned to be loving and clear in our relationships. Many of us have unrealistic images of how to love and be loved, so we frequently fall victim to our lack of knowledge and our unreal expectations. Even passionate and well-meaning couples tend to bicker and blame. Intimacy is among the most valuable experiences in life, and yet opportunities for real love are finite. Couples need a safe and sacred space to feel, to bond, to argue, to love and to evolve.

This book offers step-by-step instructions about creating the ground rules that allow a couple to create and sustain safety, love, passion and more. *Real Relationship* provides a map with much-needed sign-posts that can help couples to realize certain dreams ... and possibly to let go of others. There will, of course, be blasts from the past. Conflicts are unavoidable. It's important to feel and to express feelings in order to build vibrant relationships, but it's not okay to hurt others. Safety is paramount, so stop, look and listen. It's always important to remember that your significant other is your friend and not your enemy. There are ghosts from the past that will muck up the present. Jealousy and insecurity exist, so be sure to deal with them before they deal with you. Otherwise you may kill the thing you love, or your love may turn to stone.

Beyond this, *Real Relationship* offers suggestions about when to speak up and when to not say a word ... how to extend love and how to fight fairly ... and how and why we all need to release and reveal our pain and anger. It's better to brainstorm than bicker, and it's also better to check things out than act things out. And it's best of all to join forces and work together to find transcendent solutions. Together, couples can disarm some of the unconscious forces that would otherwise drive them apart.

We all have feet of clay, but a relationship should never become a war of attrition. There are times in every long-term relationship when serious old feelings erupt and seem to threaten our future. But we needn't allow emotional ignorance or unconscious pain to destroy our lives or our relationships. Couples can commit to learning the skills that enable them to feel the hurting, to feel together, and to find ways that allow their love to triumph over pain, over distance, over apathy or over boredom. Real love is good, deep feelings are transformative, and clear communication is the key.

Dr. Stephen Khamsi
Glen Ellen, California

Contents

FOREWORD iii

AN INTRODUCTORY FABLE: 1
Relationships are like a backpacking trip

LAST THINGS FIRST: 5
Co-create a vision of where you'd like to be

PART I: Relationships are hard, hard work 15

CHAPTER ONE: Must biology be destiny? 17

CHAPTER TWO: How expectations undermine our relationships 31

CHAPTER THREE:
The Mumdaddy: Ghosts from the Past 53

PART II: Emergency First Aid 67

CHAPTER FOUR: Stop! 69

CHAPTER FIVE: Look! 87

CHAPTER SIX: Listen! 103

PART III: Feelings 129

CHAPTER SEVEN: Attending to your feelings 131

CHAPTER EIGHT: Feeling through on your own 147

CHAPTER NINE: Working through feelings with a partner 165

PART IV: Compassionate Communication 181

CHAPTER TEN: Effective Verbal Communication 183

CHAPTER ELEVEN: Straight Talk 197

CHAPTER TWELVE: Successful Negotiation: Constructive Conflict 223

AFTERWORD 243

APPENDIX: How to find a good therapist 245

BIBLIOGRAPHY 249

AN INTRODUCTORY FABLE

The map is not the territory.
–R.D. Laing

Few of us come into marriage counseling when we are feeling good about our relationships. We usually stagger in hurting, disoriented, and feeling like failures. As one client put it to me, "Everyone else has a good relationship—why can't I? What's *wrong* with me?" The reality is that just about *everyone* has trouble with relationships, for some very good reasons. What I want to assure you of first is that you aren't a bad or inadequate person because you're relationship-challenged.

To make this idea clearer, let's take a brief trip in our imaginations. Imagine that you and your partner, in your happiest days, are going to take a backpacking trip together up to a lake high in the mountains that your parents—all four or more of them—have been telling you about for years. They've told you many times how beautiful the lake is with its soft green duff and stately pines, nestled like a blue gem in a granite cirque surrounded by tall snowcapped peaks beyond. The lake, they say, is teeming with rainbow trout just waiting to leap into your frying pan. Your dear parents even have a map to the lake and what they assure you is plenty of equipment for your hike.

Your parents pack your equipment for you. Much of it is well-used, having been handed down from their parents to them. You head out on a sunny day under a cerulean sky. You are hiking along beside a singing stream on a clearly-marked trail that follows a gentle upgrade beneath sweet-smelling bay laurel trees. You hold hands and sing hiking songs together. All's right with the world.

The first challenge comes a few miles up the trail when you arrive at a signpost indicating a trail junction that's not on your map. Hmm. Well, it looks from the map that you ought to bear to the right, so you choose that trail. Then you notice that the sun has disappeared and the once-blue sky is turning dark with thunderheads. You look in your packs for ponchos and discover that your helpful parents neglected to include them. When it begins to rain you are soon soaked through. And the one warm place on your shivering body, the back of your heel, is now blistering. You stop to put on a band aid and find none in the rather inadequate first aid kit, but there are some dry socks.

The trail is becoming steeper and rockier, the rain a torrent, the blister pops and you feel that a red-hot needle is being jabbed into your heel with every step. You come to a bit of a flat spot and try to erect your tent, but your parents forgot to put in the poles. Soon you are yelling at one another, feeling miserable, and wishing you'd never begun this adventure.

Sound familiar? That's where we find ourselves in our relationships. We begin with intoxicating visions of a Promised Land, but our maps are incomplete and the equipment our families packed us up with is inadequate. When we're miserable we take it out on each other and think of ourselves as failures.

How can we expect ourselves to be good at relationship when we lack accurate maps and equipment? In fact, in contemporary American culture, we are set up for failure. One part of us knows this, simply from the statistics of failure in relationship. But we don't want to believe that maybe it's not that we have trouble with relationships so much as that relationships have trouble with us.

• • •

Back to our backpacking trip. Let's further imagine that you have your cell phone along and have the number of a good marriage counselor. You place the call and soon hear the flutter of helicopter blades. When the copter lands nearby, you find it loaded with helpful equipment—a complete set of tent poles, excellent raingear, more comfortable shoes, and an accurate map. You towel off and put on dry clothing, toss your old gear in the copter, don your raingear, and pitch your tent. Warm and dry inside your shelter, you actually enjoy the sound of the raindrops on the tent walls. You fire up the butane stove to brew a mug of hot chocolate and decide that things aren't so bad after all. From the weather report you know the rain will abate and that tomorrow will be sunny and warm. Guided by your good map, you'll be able to find your way to the lake, though now you no longer expect that the rainbow trout will leap into your frying pan. You're gaining some wisdom. In your new wisdom you apologize to one another for being so cranky, then snuggle up in the blissful warmth of your down sleeping bags.

The great majority of us—96% by some estimates[1]—are raised in families that do not model or teach good relationship skills. We then suffer through an educational system that teaches us to sit silently in straight rows doing boring and often meaningless tasks that have little or no connection to our actual lives. Why should

1 Virginia Satir, *Peoplemaking* (1972) p. 18.

we expect that we would do well in a relationship? And yet we do expect to do well—which is a big part of the problem, for we become the victims of our expectations.

The purpose of this book is to help you sort through the archaic equipment your culture has burdened you with and to replace much of it with some that will actually work. The goal is to construct a real relationship rather than a fantasy one. Let's begin by taking a look at your map of relationship.

LAST THINGS FIRST: Co-create a vision of where you'd like to be

The end is where we start from.
–T.S. Eliot

Let's begin with a vision of the place you can come to in your relationship. I will model that vision on what I know—my relationship of over two decades with Yashi. You should know that it took us about ten years to get there, but more about that later.

You will notice that I have highlighted partings and reconnections. These are of particular importance to every relationship.

A Day in the Life

A morning person, Yashi usually is up, meditating and doing yoga, long before I stir. When she is finished she brews us a pot of tea. I usually get up when I hear the crockery clink. We greet each other with a "Good morning!" and a hug and kiss. I am filled with gratitude, first, that I have lived to see another beautiful day and, next, that I can share my life with such a wonderful woman. I feel a deep sense of quiet joy just seeing her each morning. We sit with our tea to check in with one another and share our dreams of the previous night. What we are finding fascinating lately is that our dreams often have a common theme: Yesterday morning both of us were in Paris. The morning connection takes from ten minutes to an hour. Then we breakfast together.

In our household we both earn the money and we both share the common chores. For instance, we each cook and clean up from the same number of meals in a given week. This morning I make us each a quarter of a papaya with a wedge of lime and hot oatmeal with yogurt and walnuts. Yashi does the bulk of the cleaning up. There is a kind of dance that we do in our kitchen, interweaving bodies and tasks as we prepare meals or clean them up, that I find soothing. Over breakfast we share our plans for the day and brainstorm any logistical issues, such as who will call and meet with the guy who's going to give us a bid on a new furnace.

"Will you meet with Randy about the new heater?" Yashi asks me. "You're so much better at that sort of thing."

I sigh.

"Flattery will get you whatever you want, Sweet Lips."

There's an embarrassingly large part of me which dislikes having to deal with mundane matters like the furnace. I judge them as less important than my writing, my clients, my children, or my relationship. This judgment leads to irritation. I often wish I were wealthy enough to hire an administrative assistant—or have a nice Mommy—to handle all the mundane for me.

So I get to practice acceptance and non-judgment, reminding myself that in the overall order of things the furnace is just as important—and unimportant—as this book. Occasionally, I succeed in this difficult practice. More often, I get grumpy, and Yashi says, "Are you getting grumpy, honey?" I then need to practice moving the grumps out.

After our morning meetings, I retreat to my study to write on this book for a couple hours. Yashi goes up to the office to see clients. Whenever we part, we make a point of connecting briefly for a kiss and a "Goodbye, sweetheart!" We never take it for granted that we will see each other again but try to live totally in the present. We are poignantly aware that every parting is a foreshadowing of the one that will mark our separation in this life. We find this awareness helps us value the precious quality of each moment together.

When I go up to the office (a three minute walk up our wooded hill), I often see Yashi briefly as we cross paths there. We might exchange a bit of business—"Jennifer can't make group tomorrow night"—and a touch. Then she's out the door to meet a friend for a walk and lunch. I work for two hours, then return to the house for lunch on my own. At lunchtime I like to read the newspapers. With a cup of coffee in hand, I return to the office for another two hours of clients. During my first hour I smile as Yashi whizzes by in her blue road rocket. I guess she'll probably start working in her garden and harvesting some spinach and cucumbers for dinner. After I'm finished work for the day and have made my calls, I drive down to the softball field to play a game or two with my buddies. Often there is a postgame celebration that features ice-cold beer along with bad jokes and good camaraderie. I feel a lot of gratitude toward Yashi that she freely makes room for my buddy time. I think of it as my men's group.

When I return home as the sun is setting over our western hills, I bellow "Billy's home!" as I barge through the door. My parents kept telling me not to be a "bull in a china shop" but I never mastered the art. "Billy" was my childhood nickname and my current *nom de jeu* on the softball field. I look into her study to find Yashi talking to her son on the phone. She waves one hand toward me. I come up behind her and gently touch her neck, whisper, "Say hi for me," then head to the shower.

After I'm cleaned up, I pour us each a glass of wine and we go out onto the deck to watch the last colors of the sunset. We each take a few minutes to recount our day and the state of soul we find ourselves in at the moment. Yashi listens patiently as I exaggerate my athletic exploits and explain how miserable I feel when I drop a fly ball. She tells me what her son is up to and their plans for getting together in Vancouver. Then we go in to sit down to the Cobb salad she's prepared for us, where we continue our conversation. After the dishes are done, we carry a cup of tea to our reading area, where we take turns reading from our current book to one another. At bedtime, we make it a point to say "Goodnight" and to have some physical contact before turning in. I will often stay up later, reading or playing my computer game, but I never miss the goodnight part.

Is Love Boring?

That's a typical day for us. You'll notice that we interweave time together with time apart. We also have a One True Love day, which happens every Wednesday and has some very special features, including the opportunity to make love, and Soul Day, during which we don't even speak. Like many couples, we also usually include a Date Night each week when we go out for dinner and some event (movie, play, music), but we see that as less important to our relationship than the aforementioned days. Then again, we no longer have children around, so we have plenty of time to relate one-on-one without interruption. For couples with children, Date Night is a chance to get off by yourselves as a couple. We spend a minimum of fifteen hours a week intimately together.

Also like most couples, we have our frictions at times. However, while we had our share of those in the past, we find they occur less frequently now and we are able to move through them fairly efficiently when they do arise. We estimate that about 90% of the time we are feeling good together. Because we both value serenity and inner peace, we each use a variety of practices to foster that state. Because we have learned how to communicate fairly effectively and to negotiate differences constructively, we trust that any challenge that we face will be an opportunity for growing together rather than an iceberg for the *Titanic* of relationship. Consequently, we no longer panic when we encounter such a challenge.

We cultivate a peaceful life. We've chosen to live in a relatively quiet area a mile out of town, where we are surrounded by forest and out of sight of any human neighbors. There are lots of birds and squirrels, a herd of deer, a bobcat and a family of bears. This morning we saw two beautiful coyotes catch a squirrel. We live modestly in a small house we have paid off. We carry no debt. We have no TV reception and we screen our calls.

For a couple of weeks each winter, we'll be snowed in without electricity. We hunker down by the wood stove and read by lantern-light. Only our hardiest clients are willing to hike in to the office for their sessions. Otherwise, our lives aren't that different from normal.

We seldom attend large and noisy gatherings any more, other than our children's or clients' weddings. Occasionally, we'll get together with good friends for dinner and conversation or a swim in the river. A blowout for us is margaritas and fajitas at the local sports bar when we want to watch a World Cup game or the Olympics with friends who also lack TV.

Certainly such a bucolic life is mediated to some extent by our age, though I think more significantly by our state of being in our relationship. We have calmed the innate fidget of our youth with the balm of a deep and abiding loving connection. I realize that much of the frenetic peregrination of my younger days was searching behavior. I was prospecting the wide world for a heart of gold. Having found what we were looking for, we now cultivate repose.

I can imagine some of you thinking, at this point, "Boy, that sure sounds boring!"Certainly, in relationship as with shoes, one size will not fit all. I confess that I myself probably would have made such a judgment at 25 or 30, when I was traveling the world and meeting beautiful, exotic women while surviving close calls in war zones. As I cruise through the backside of my sixties I find that I am more interested in the bluebird couple feeding new chicks than the fight over fixing the economy. We do change with the aging process. I don't mean to imply that anyone should expect to lose a vivid sexual relationship, which, I am happy to report, will continue within a loving twosome. But I do think that one comes to a quite different understanding of what Love is and is not.

We grow up in a culture that identifies love largely with the in-love state, which is a temporary euphoria provoked by a cascade of powerful biochemicals, usually accompanied by or followed by the painful drama of the love/hate relationship with its jealousy, frustration, disappointment, and despair. How many movies, plays, and popular songs dwell upon one side or the other of this state? You can run the gamut from *Romeo and Juliet* to the "she done me wrong" ballads of country music. In drama and intensity of feeling, both the in-love state and its tragic aftermath can be extremely alluring. We can easily become addicted to the chemical cocktail and to the drama surrounding it.

Nevertheless, it will be my thesis that, seductive though this state might be, it is not true Love. We confuse the two at our peril, for if we define love as the in-love state of temporary insanity, we will never have a good, long-term relationship.

Let me attempt to describe what I believe Love can be. Any attempt to define Love, which is a part of the Great Mystery, will be inadequate. Poets, songwriters, philosophers, psychologists, and now neuroscientists have come up with excellent partial truths. I will try to do so, with great humility, by contrasting Love with the other experience, which we might call "longing." Please understand that I don't pretend to have the last word on Love—and I sincerely doubt that anyone ever will.

Longing is transitory. Love is eternal.
Love is warm and easy. Longing runs hot and cold and struggles.
Longing is focused on what I can get out of the relationship. Love on what is best for my partner as well as myself. Love is thus considerate.
Love accepts what is. Longing attempts to manipulate and change. It is continually discontent.
Love is kind. Longing can be agitated and angry.
Longing is fearful of loss. Love knows that our connection in Source is eternal.
Longing seeks to possess. Love sets up no walls.
In longing, we find ourselves worse than we imagined. In Love, better.

The Mystery of Love defies encapsulation in mere words, for it is larger than language. My words are only weathered signposts pointing toward the country of Love. Although even in a mostly longing relationship one might experience occasional flashes of Love, he or she will always be brought back to the ultimate pain that underlies all addiction. Longing is an addiction. Love is the release from addiction.

What Kind of Relationship Do You Want?

I offer this glimpse into our relationship not to imply that you should be like us but to stir your own creative juices so you might envision the kind of relationship you would like for yourself. I invite you to take a few minutes with the following exercise, which requires a pencil and a piece of paper, to begin the process of envisioning where you will end up.

Exercise

Ground your vision in the particulars of a normal day: What do you do when you first awake? When do you spend time together? In what way? With what tone do you speak to one another? How do you express affection? When and how do you make love? How do you organize around other important people, such as children and family and friends? Do you formally say goodbye when you part? When and in what ways do you reconnect in the evening? How? When and how do you say goodnight? Visualize specifics.

Then you might want to make some notes on what you've envisioned. As you write down the particulars of how you would ideally relate, rate each behavior with a number between 1 and 10, with 1 meaning "very important" and 10 meaning "nice, but not very important." You can put down as many ones or fives or whatever as you wish.

If you're with a partner who's willing to do so, you might want to ask them to do the same exercise, separately. When they've finished, you can place your two visions side by side to begin to work toward a shared vision. You might each find something in the other's notes that you'd like to add to yours. Copying off each other's work is actually encouraged.

Finally, go through your visions and underline those particulars that you think would be difficult to manifest.

Here's the beginning of such an exercise from Judy and Sam:

Judy	Sam
1 Cuddle when we wake up	1 Make love when we wake up
3 Eat breakfast together	2 Take a shower together
1 Say "I love you"	5 Read the paper together
2 Hug and kiss goodbye	4 Judy packs my lunch
4 Sam calls me during the day	2 Judy doesn't bug me at work
3 Sam takes me to lunch some days	5 Judy cleans the house for us

And so on.

Congratulations! You now have your own map of where you are headed. I suggest that you refer to it frequently—perhaps even put it on the refrigerator door where you can see it daily. There is a lot of research to show that we tend to become what we imagine we can be. I love the study that demonstrated that a random group of high school basketball players who visualized shooting free throws for fifteen minutes after practice every day for two weeks improved their free throw shooting as much as those who shot free throws for the extra time.

Here's a quote to speed you on your way:

Whatever you can do, or dream you can do, begin it.
The moment one definitely commits oneself then providence
moves too. Boldness has genius, power, and magic in it.

–Johan Wolfgang von Goethe

PART I: WHY ARE RELATIONSHIPS SO *HARD* NOWADAYS?

Relationships have never been easy, at least not after the first couple of years. Xantippe emptied a chamberpot over the wisest head in Athens because she was angry that her husband Socrates preferred seeking knowledge to amassing wealth. Shakespeare's star-cross'd lovers end up suicides. Anna Karenina throws herself beneath the wheels of a locomotive. In fact, one can make a good case that the central theme of Western Lit is of one unhappy and usually disastrous relationship after another from Helen of Troy's ship-launching infidelity down to our screen stars' latest peccadilloes in today's tabloid.

And, though there are differences in the way Occident and Orient perceive them, the oldest novel we know of, written by a Japanese woman, is a story of painful relationships.

While relationships have always presented challenges, I think most of us would agree that the particular difficulties of our times place an added burden upon couples. Several of those vectors you can list as readily as I, through simple observation or by reading the popular magazines. You might cite our mobile society, gender differences, the loss of traditional roles, or our deficiency in communication skills. In this section we are going to examine the three challenges to relating that are the most significant: Our biology, our expectations, and what I call the Mumdaddy, the ghosts of the past.

What I'd encourage you to do as you read is not to be overwhelmed by these challenges but to become more compassionate toward yourself and your partner for the very hard work you have already done in dealing with them. As we develop a compassionate curiosity about ourselves and our partners in relationships and accumulate more understanding, we will find that our capacities for toleration and acceptance grow. Our relationships are our primary opportunity for us to grow into better people, specifically into people who are more compassionate, kinder, and more accepting.

That is the ultimate promise of real relationship.

This section is an important informational background for what follows, but if you're in a lot of pain right now, skip ahead to Part II and apply the emergency tools you will find there.

1: MUST BIOLOGY BE DESTINY?

Biology is destiny.
–Sigmund Freud

Susan and Eddie came in for therapy after they'd already decided to divorce, thinking I might be able to work a miracle or, more likely, that they'd use the sessions to part amicably. They were an attractive young couple without any children, both with demanding careers. They'd been married for three years.

"We've just lost that loving feeling," Eddie said. "It's like it flew out the window."

"We do love each other," Susan added. "We're just not *in love* anymore. Do you know what I mean?"

I said that I did. I hear some version of this story every week.

Recent breakthroughs in neuroscience have shed important understanding on one rather momentous reason we are so relationship-challenged. When we "fall in love," neuroscientists[2] tell us, a "cocktail" of biochemicals is triggered within our brains. Some of these chemicals are dopamine, serotonin, norepinephrine, vasopressin, and oxytocin. We quite literally get high. We feel euphoric, as if "walking on air," and we can become addicted to the love object who is triggering this chemical cascade within us and/or to the chemicals themselves. These chemicals increase exponentially for about six months and then begin to gradually deplete over the next couple years.

Let's look at the first year, when we are literally drugged. In that state we *know* that whatever old fools say, they are just wrong and out of touch with true love. The way we feel will last forever. The person we are in love with is perfect for us and probably the best human being ever to walk the earth. During this stage people do crazy things, including writing love songs and poems that celebrate this state that let the rest of us know (or remember) how sweet it is. It is certainly one of the most profound experiences a human being can have. We want it to last forever. We hope it will. We don't see why it shouldn't. Even the skeptical French shout, "*Vive l'amour!*" We enshrine it with those ideals and speak of Soul Mates. We are certain that, like swans, people are meant to mate for life. Where does this belief originate?

Plato explained it by the story of the Bifurcated Beings.

Plato's Allegory

We were all once, Plato said, beings with two heads and four arms and four legs, but we got chopped in half. Our skin was then pulled tightly over the raw wound and fastened at the belly button.

---

2 The most accessible discussions I have found are in Helen Fisher, *Why We Fall in Love* (1992) and in *A General Theory of Love* (2000) by Thomas Lewis, Fari Amini, and Richard Lannon.

(Obviously this is true, because we have belly buttons to prove it.) Okay, so now we're half-beings with one head and two arms and two legs running around looking for our "other half." When we finally find him or her and join our bodies in love-making we once again become two-headed, four-armed beings, and we have that blissful feeling that we are whole once again.

A silly myth? Of course, but one that points out an important psychological truth: As separate beings we tend to feel incomplete and we seek out a partner with whom we will feel whole again. Another way of looking at Plato's tale is that it is true—when we were in our mother's uterus we *did* have two heads—our own and hers. In the womb we felt a sense of blissful union with An Other, a feeling we seek to recreate in our present love relationships, hoping to reconstruct that lost Eden.

A huge part of most of us longs for a blissful union with one other human being. Every culture on the planet celebrates this desire. For instance, in a wedding ceremony we promise to forsake all others and stay together till death do us part.

We may scoff at Plato's origin of the belly button but most of us take as given beliefs such as: There is One destined for each of us. When we find him or her, we will be blissfully happy, mostly, forever. We won't be powerfully attracted to anyone else and will remain faithful to our mate. Each of these beliefs is true—during the love cocktail phase of the relationship.

We Identify a Chemical Madness as 'Love'

Part of our problem with relationships is that we have inflated expectations based upon a temporary chemical imbalance that feels really good most of the time and the messages of the love songs and poetry written by people in this demented state. We believe this feeling will, or should, last forever. Upon it, and upon the considerable body of poetry and myth that has grown up out of it, we have fashioned some very high ideals.[3] These ideals manifest one part of our nature. There are, however, some other parts which we ignore at our peril.

There is a dark side to this imbalance, for instance. People in its grip will act pretty crazy sometimes, not only writing poetry but also killing themselves, their soul mates, or their real or imagined rivals. What is happening in us with this massive infusion of chemicals that makes us act differently than we do for most of the rest of our lives?

Let's step back to examine the larger biological story. Mother Nature has developed a powerful biochemical means of getting people (and, one would suppose, all animals) to come together, to mate, and to produce new generations. To do that effectively, she needs us to fall in love, enter a state of temporary insanity, have lots of sex for a while, and then stick around for long enough for the baby to be born and breastfed. Human beings with their huge heads need an extended period of gestation outside the womb that gazelles, for instance, don't. Gazelles can run within a few hours. They become independent quickly. Babies can't even walk for a year.

But once Baby has been breastfed for a year or so and is scurrying about bipedally, Ma Nature has other plans that run counter to our high ideals. She's interested in producing life that's most likely to survive and to pass on more life. It's not in her best interests for the same pair bond to keep producing children with very similar genetic structures. More of a woman's offspring will survive if they have different genes. So she tapers off the love cocktail for Mate 1 and gets ready to retrigger it for Mate 2.

Let's look at it from Ma Nature's perspective:

---

3 Denis de Rougemont in *Love in the Western World* (1940) and C.S. Lewis in *The Allegory of Love* (1948) make a brilliant case that the very beliefs we have about love are conditioned by the romantic poetry of the troubadour love songs which were actually disguised religious heresies speaking not about human love but about love of the Divine.

"These stupid *Homo sapiens* would probably die out if I didn't juice them up enough to get over their self-centered orneriness. So I'll squirt them full of some chemicals that make them gaga about the next histocompatible being who comes along and even dispose them to have lots of sex. That'll bond them tightly and make pregnancy more likely. Okay, that'll take roughly 9-15 months. But with Mommy breastfeeding, it'd be good to keep Pops around to bring in the bacon for another year or so. Can't have starving children and Mom'll need help for awhile. Her hormones are already changing around birth and breastfeeding, which will also act as a form of birth control—I don't want the offspring too close together, for they're then less likely to survive. She's already less interested in sex with him. But we need him to stick a bit longer. Hmm. I'll keep him somewhat juiced so he'll stay attached for at least another year, till Junior is walking and Mom is free to start gathering fruits and roots again. Then I'll phase out both of their love cocktails. They'll wonder why they were ever attracted to each other. Soon they'll find themselves more interested in new partners with different genes—I want as much diversity as I can make, for diversity survives. Too bad about the silly ideals they've manufactured based on the prior two-and-a-half years, but they'll get over them when I hit them with the next blast of Love Potion #9."

In fact, at about the two-and-a-half year mark, give or take, the chemical bonding that was so powerful at six months that she didn't care if he burped in public has pretty much run out of attractant. When do most divorces occur? At the three-year mark.[4]

4 This statistic comes from countries in which marriage is based upon romantic love. In countries with a high percentage of arranged marriages, the divorce rate peaks at six months. If your parents have put you together with someone you really can't stand, you know that pretty quickly.

These are the facts. There is also much theorizing based upon these facts.

In the state of Nature, anthropologists hypothesize, the former "soul mates" are drawn to new "soul mates," and mate in a serial manner. They may well retain a fond connection, which further assists the mother's offspring, for even if Mate 1 is off with a new paramour he'll probably still drop off an extra wildebeest steak now and again for the old family. A woman with many such mates then not only has offspring with quite varied genetic structures more likely to survive the next plague, they're also better fed and thus more likely to live long enough to pass on their own genes.

So, the theory is, we come from a long line of philanderers. In fact current research demonstrates that every society on the planet, even those that punish it with death, is rife with adultery. The last statistic I read indicated that two in three people of both genders in long term relationships in the U.S. have had at least one sexual experience outside the primary relationship that they're willing to admit to anonymously. In other words, adultery is *normal.*

We Have a Problem

The big problem, of course, is that we have two contradictory systems operating within us simultaneously: Biologically, we are oriented toward sequential and usually overlapping relationships. Psychologically, most of us hunger for one person with whom to bond deeply and share a lifetime.

One solution, of course, would be for us to let go of our psychological needs and to accept that we are going to go through a series of intense mating relationships, at least in our childbearing years, changing partners without rancor about every three years. If you look around with a clear eye, you will note that such behavior is actually going on anyway, except with lots of rancor. There is a problem with this method, however. Children seem to really like having both their parents together and on hand. Generally, they don't like having to adapt to a stream of new step-parents, even with the extra wildebeest steaks. You will hear people who've run out of love cocktail say they're staying together "for the children." There is a virtue in that.

On the other hand, I've certainly become much less judgmental toward our human tendency to be drawn to more than a single soul mate, a familiar story that hits the newsstands on a weekly basis. Up until the biochemical research was done, most people, myself included, tended to believe that unless you conformed to the ideal of one mate per person per lifetime, there was something wrong with you, morally, spiritually, physically, and/or psychologically. I hope that we can shed that cruel perspective. I would like to see us be more accepting of our human inheritance by understanding what Mother Nature is trying to accomplish. We need to know and grasp the significance of her plan. Then we can make more conscious decisions based upon what we know about ourselves, our partners, and our mutual dreams.

Now put yourself, imaginatively, in the shoes of someone who's experiencing love cocktail depletion syndrome. First, you're not quite so high. You're beginning to lose that expansive feeling. You actually start to see things differently. You begin to see your partner not as an idealized being who can do no wrong but as rather imperfect. Whereas before you were amazed by how similar you were ("Golly, I never found anyone else who loves horses the way I do!"), you become gradually aware of how different you actually are ("You mean you only took up riding so you could get to know me?!") When he burps in public you now are irritated. When she wears that hat you used to think was cute, you find yourself embarrassed. Avoiders start wanting more "space." You remember you used to like to play tennis or have lunch with your girlfriends. There are more arguments, often over petty issues. Then you patch it back up, especially when a good night follows a good fight. However, you are already on the slippery slope and you find yourselves spiraling downward. You start to wonder whether you are really meant for each other. Maybe, you think, we've made a mistake.

Relationships Go Through Predictable Stages

This is a predictable stage in every relationship. It even has a name: Differentiation.[5] In the first, Romantic, stage, you are intensely bonding, like a mother with her newborn child. Now Mom's tired of being tied down so much and toddler wants to explore the world but still wants Mommy there. Each must learn to adjust to this new stage. The same is true for any coupleship.

Usually one person takes the role of the Differentiator. In their first session Susan said, "I need more space to breathe and be myself! I'm going to get back into acting. My ex-husband Joe offered me a part in his new play that I just can't pass up. It's just what I need in my career."

The other partner usually panics and clings. Even though a part of him may be ready for a little more space, this is way too much too fast. It was for Eddie, who said, "But if you're rehearsing every night, when will we have time together? You'll be spending more time with Joe than you will with me!"

Jealousy can rear its ugly head. There are fights over time and space. Susan felt boxed in and angry (and guilty about that) while Eddie felt abandoned and terrified. Tears and recriminations flow.

5 For a lucid study of the stages that every relationship that lasts long enough goes through, see Bader and Pearson, *In Quest of the Mythical Mate: A Developmental Approach to Diagnosis and Treatment in Couples Therapy* (1988).

Finally Susan uttered those fateful words, "Maybe we're just not meant for each other."

Every coupleship must negotiate this challenging stage, in which it is moving from the magical temporary insanity of the Romantic stage, when everything seems to flow so easily, to the grating difficulties of the Differentiation stage, when everything seems so hard. The tasks of Differentiation that I passed on to Eddie and Susan are to:

1. Accept that you are different people with different needs
2. Be able to express your needs to each other without blaming
3. Develop a healthy "fight style" to negotiate your needs
4. Rebalance togetherness with apartness
5. Stop the Blame Game
6. Accept that you must deal with the diminishing love cocktail.

Differentiation doesn't mean you are falling out of love. It means your relationship is growing into a new place. There will be some growing pains. The question you need put to yourself is, "Am I willing to do the hard work to birth this relationship into another stage, or would I rather just let it go and find another partner to start all over with?"

Two Radical Alternatives

There are, I should say in all honesty, two radical alternatives to keeping passion alive which many people end up choosing, usually unconsciously. I should warn you that they lack societal approval at this time. The first of these, which we might call the Create An

Obstacle approach, is perhaps best exemplified by the old troubadour love poem, *The Romance of Tristan and Iseult.*[6]

King Mark sends his beloved nephew, Tristan, to Ireland to fetch his young bride-to-be, Iseult. Tristan carries with him a love potion, sealed in a horn, that he is instructed to give to Iseult to quaff just before she meets Mark. But when Tristan and Iseult are dying of thirst, lost at sea, they decide to drink the potion (Love Cocktail) themselves, with predictable results. By the time they miraculously make landfall they are in love and Iseult is no longer a virgin.

Do they fess up? Of course not. They fulfill expectations and Iseult marries her betrothed, Mark. But of course Tristan and she find ways of continuing their secret and now adulterous love with creative ingenuity.

When King Mark finally and reluctantly sees that they are betraying him, rather than killing them, as his councilors advise, he banishes them from the court. They wander out into the forest together. Now, you might think that they'd be happy as larks, together at last in a state of nature. Just the opposite: They lose their passion for each other when the love cocktail wears off and *there are no longer any obstacles to their relationship*. Tristan places his sword between them when they sleep, as a symbol of such obstacles and their belated chastity. He tries to talk Iseult into begging Mark for forgiveness—he feels guilty that her dresses are in tatters and she can no longer order sweetmeats.

On a hunting trip into the greenwood, King Mark sees them sleeping on their blanket, the sword gleaming between them. He decides that he has wrongly accused them and grants them a reprieve. As soon as they are back in the castle, with the former obstacles to their passion in place, their passion returns and they return to passionate sex.

---

6 As retold by Joseph Bedier and translated by Hilaire Belloc (1945).

If you want to know the rest of the story, you'll have to read the book. The point for us here is that people have recognized for a long time that keeping passion alive is a difficult agenda. In fact, according to Andreas Capellanus, who wrote *The Art of Courtly Love* back in the twelfth century, Eleanor of Aquitaine assembled the women of the French nobility at the "Court of Love" in Poitiers where they decreed that love (by which they meant romantic passion) and marriage were incompatible. One could only, they agreed, be romantically passionate about someone outside the marriage: A lover who was a sometime thing and from whom you were separated by obstacles.

How discouraging for some of us. How delightful for others.

The truth contained in both this decree and in the great poem of the troubadours is that romantic passion is challenged by living in a three-bedroom split level home while paying taxes and changing diapers. We know this truth already. We know that someone outside the relationship, who doesn't have oatmeal spilled on his or her suit, can seem more alluring. A lover from whom we are separated by various obstacles can remain alluring. I have had more than one client who kept falling in love only with someone who was already married. I have had others who came to relish the fact that their partner's occupation kept them separated for big chunks of time.

I think that what's important is that each of us becomes more aware of what form of relationship we really want.

Open Relationship/Polyamory

Another possible solution to the problem of wanting to have a long-term primary relationship while simultaneously being able to have sexual variety is what was called "open marriage" in the 70s after a book of that title and has re-surfaced recently under the name of polyamory, literally, "loving many." Since I have written elsewhere on this topic,[7] I will here simply note that while I have the utmost respect for those who are attempting to solve our chemical problem openly and honestly. I can say from a personal experience of seven years in such a relationship that maintaining one takes an enormous amount of time and energy. Because of the strong feelings triggered by sexual jealousy in our culture, most people find it daunting to attempt to balance two or more relationships at the same time in an open and caring manner. To the nay-sayers who carp that it cannot be done, I would reply that many have done so, quite successfully, for a period of time much longer than most conventional relationships last. Personally, I really liked both the freedom and the honesty of that lifestyle. I learned a lot about relating and became a much better person through the experience.

Nonetheless, I chose to move back to monogamy, for three reasons. First, I wanted to free up time for other things, like writing books and raising children. Second, I didn't want to inflict that lifestyle upon my children. Third, I wanted to go as deeply as I could possibly go with one other human being and to see what I came to in that venture.

So I came to the central question of this book: How can we overcome these biological imperatives and preserve a healthy, vivid, real relationship?

Some final thoughts

Just remember this: How you feel in the first two or three years toward a lover will not last forever. That's a biological truth. But, although biology need not be destiny, you will need to accept the reality that you will not feel the same way you did at first. Then, you

7 "Striking the Roots of Sexual Jealousy," *City Miner* I, 1, 1976.

will need to avoid making up the story that "I just don't love you anymore." Or, more commonly, as Susan said to Eddie, "I love you but I'm not 'in love' with you."

What those statements translate to is "I'm no longer drunk on the love cocktail." Love, however, can be more than the cocktail. It can be the whole feast.

My experience is that once we are able to love someone, which we might briefly (and inadequately) define as caring about their well-being as much as we do about our own, we can always return to that place. We can move past biology and expectations and life frustrations and all the other challenges to relationship and come back to our deep caring.

If what you really want is the intoxication of what people call the "in love" state, then you will necessarily move through a series of partners or conduct an illicit affair beset by obstacles. Please be clear about this. It does not mean you are a bad person. It means you value the intoxication of the love cocktail more than you value the benefits of having one partner. Robert Palmer will sing to you, "Might as well face it, you're addicted to love." You can certainly tell yourself that you are in alignment with Nature's plan.

If what you want is a long-term relationship with one person without the complexities of other lovers, open or secret, you will need to understand why the feelings change, grieve and accept their loss, and shift your focus to what you can do about building a deep and abiding love that will include retriggerings of the old ecstatic feelings. The purpose of this book is to make that state available to you, if you choose to accept the mission.

Recent research into what is called *epigenetics*[8] holds an exciting new possibility. Although most of us were taught that who we are is pretty much determined by either our genes or our environment,

---

8 See, for instance, Lipton & Bhaerman, *Spontaneous Evolution: Our Positive Future (And A Way To Get There From Here)* (2009).

Nature or Nurture, cutting edge science is demonstrating that the environmental field and our genes interact—who we are impacts the environment and the environment we are in turns certain genes on or off. So, while we may well be under the influence of the philandering gene, we also have the capacity to mute that tendency and to activate our capacity for a deeper love.

In short, we need not be prisoners of our biological destiny. We can accept biological reality, rather than clinging to an unreal illusion and thereby making ourselves miserable, and also accept our power to create the life we want. As we do so, what we begin is the process of freeing ourselves from the expectations that narrow our lives, as we shall examine in more detail in the next chapter.

2: HOW EXPECTATIONS UNDERMINE RELATIONSHIPS

I am not here to live up to your expectations;
And you are not here to live up to mine.
–Fritz Perls

If I expect that when you read this book you will immediately send me a congratulatory letter and include me in your patronage for promising writers, I will probably experience a great deal of disappointment. If you expect that you will always be high on the Love Cocktail, you *will* be disappointed. And yet we bring similar inflated mindsets to our relationships, expecting our partners to behave in the ways we think they "should" or that we would like. Many of these expectations are formed in childhood, as we shall see in the next chapter, and more are added during the Romantic stage of relating. We then end up disappointed in our partners and often frustrated with them, and they feel disappointed and frustrated that they cannot seem to please. Consequently, hurt feelings and then resentments are likely to form on both sides.

When Sally and Ian came into my office they were ready to break up. They had been together a bit over a year and had planned to have children, but now they could barely look at each other. The immediate cause of their upset was the fact that Ian, while vacuuming the kitchen floor, had used an attachment that Sally judged would surely scratch the wood. There was a part of me, I blush to admit, that wanted to burst out laughing at the fact that they were ready to never see each other again over so seemingly petty a detail. However, many years as a couples' therapist has taught me that, as Einstein put it, God is in the details. The details, while petty, usually are but the tip of the iceberg of conscious or unconscious expectations underneath.

Ian, who presented as the unruffled, rational partner, explained that, while he knew that Sally wanted him to use her attachment because she feared his attachment would scratch the floor, he wasn't sure she was right and wanted to test her hypothesis on a small, out-of-the-way piece of flooring. He perceived her "hysterical overreaction" to his "science experiment" as evidence of her fundamental instability. He expected that she, seeing what he was doing, would simply give him the benefit of the doubt and ask him about it rather than flying off the handle "like a crazy lady." He judged that she was treating him like a child.

Sally, who was still seething, responded that she expected him to tell her what he was doing ahead of actually doing it so she could have some input. She hated it that he discounted her intelligence and treated her just like "all the men in your family treat women—like we're brainless bimbos." From experience, she knew that his attachment would scratch the woodwork. She expected Ian to value her knowledge.

"This is a larger issue in our relationship," she said. "You almost always doubt my competency or brains. You treat me like your Dad treats your Mom, and I hate it."

I could see that they were caught in so complex a web of expectations and old feelings that I hardly knew where to begin to attempt to untangle their problem. I decided to help them make their expectations conscious first and get to the feelings next.

Almost all of us are similarly entangled in a web of expectations, conscious and unconscious. It is helpful for us to acknowledge our expectations and then to decide what we want to do about them, if anything.

Categories of Expectations

While we might be aware of some of our expectations—for instance, that the sun will rise tomorrow morning—most of them are unconscious. They tend to be formed in our early experiences of loving relationships with our primary caregivers, mostly Mom and Dad. A major portion of them come from such seemingly obvious rules as, "After using the toilet, one flushes." If your partner's family didn't, you will tend to see his or her behavior as "just wrong." You may even feel disgusted. We might call these *cultural expectations*, for they arise within the culture of our families of origin and often mirror the larger culture that we grow up in.

My children grew up in California during drought years. To conserve water, the government of the state, then headed by Jerry Brown, who at the time of this writing has just assumed office again, decreed that we shouldn't be too eager to flush our toilets. The catchy mnemonic during those dry years was:

If it's yellow, let it mellow.
If it's brown, flush it down.

I think the pun was intentional.

My children grew up being taught to conserve water according to this ditty. There was a very good, green reason to do so.

They learned that one *shouldn't* flush after urinating. They no doubt still assume that restrained flushing is admirable. I can only imagine what it's like for their wives, lovely women from the wetlands of Florida and Brazil, to find a pungent yellow toilet bowl in the morning—and the discussions that follow.

This is an example of a cultural expectation that I could observe being formed from its very beginnings, when I had a heck of a time trying to retrain myself *not* to flush. Such changes, as we shall see, are not easy to achieve, even when we wish to make them for quite excellent reasons. But our brains have what neuroscientitsts call *neuroplasticity*, meaning you can teach an old dog new tricks.

As Ian and Sally's therapy progressed, it soon became evident that Ian had a cultural expectation that women weren't as logical as men. Sally's own unconscious cultural expectation was that men should defer to women's wisdom in household tasks.

Another and different set of expectations arise from what we wanted as children but didn't get. For example, Sally's parents had failed to give her the kind of valuation she deserved. She now expected Ian, her present partner, to make up for their shortcomings. In a similar manner, because Ian's father went into rages when Ian questioned his authority, Ian was left with a feeling of deprivation about being seen and valued for who he was. He wished Sally would see how smart he was being in making the scientific test in a way that wouldn't damage anything visible. We can call these *deprivation expectations*.

> Each partner will tow a whole raft of expectations, conscious and unconscious, cultural and deprivation, into the present relationship.

Let's look at a few of the more popular and dangerous expectations held by people like Sally and Ian in our culture:

I have a soulmate or "other half."
I can fall in love at first sight.
Soulmates will live happily ever after.
Soulmates will always have great sex.
He'll know what I need without me having to ask for it.
Love conquers all.
We'll be able to work out our problems through rational communication.
We'll understand each other.
We'd never hurt one another.
We'll never be attracted to someone else. If you are, you have fallen out of love with me.
If I've lost that "loving feeling" for you, it means I'm not "in love" with you any more.
We will be sexually monogamous.
If I avoid all conflict in our relationship, we'll be happy.
If I yell loud enough, I'll get my way.
Sometimes people need to be manipulated for their own good.

Exercise

I encourage you to set this book aside, find a pen and paper, and draw a vertical line down the middle of the paper. Jot down on the left side of the line as many of your expectations in relating that you can come up with in ten minutes. Ask yourself what you expect of your partner and of yourself. Put in the small ones as well as the grand ones such as the above. Do you expect your partner to tell you he loves you? Do you expect her to call you if she's running late?

Then, on the right hand side of the sheet, write in your *reactions*, in feelings and action, when that expectation is not met.

You can keep this sheet—and probably quite a few more—to add on more expectations as you become aware of them. As you do, you will gradually become more aware of how many expectations you have. Please do not judge yourself for having them—everyone does. Your task is to observe, with a sense of curiosity and acceptance, what your expectation system is, as if you were a anthropologist from another planet who wished to understand Earthlings.

I would like to emphasize this point. An especially harmful cultural expectation that most of us have grown up with is that there is a right and a wrong way to be, to feel, to do things, and to conduct relationships. For a variety of reasons that we needn't go into right now, we become very attached to such rigid systems of belief and quite distressed when reality won't conform to our expectations. We say or think, "But this is the way I or my partner or relationship *should* be!"

One couple actually broke up over the position of the lid on the toilet seat. Tamara believed that leaving the seat up allowed the *chi*, or cosmic energy, of the household to escape. Kent had trouble believing that concept and didn't like the way Tamara shrilly insisted that he should do it her way, if he didn't want her to think he was a dunce. The real issue wasn't so much whether Tamara's belief was accurate as that she was demanding. For her, down was the way it should be and had to be. When Kent couldn't follow her prescription, she would attack him verbally, calling him stupid and passive-aggressive. That's what really drove him away.

I would encourage you to be open to seeing things as they actually are—including the times and ways you beat yourself up as well as when you judge your partner for failing to do things the way you think they *should* be done.

As you begin to do so, you will notice how often you beat yourself and your partner up, psychologically, for failing to live up to your expectations, for not being who you should.

We might call this habit of mind *shoulding* upon ourselves.

The primary consequence of it is unhappiness.

> The distance between our expectations and reality is perfect measure of our unhappiness.

Reality is pretty much the way it is. It doesn't change much. The sun ariseth. The seasons change. People live and die. Toilet seats are either up or down. What we can most readily change is not reality but the expectations we attempt to impose upon it. As we release many of our impossible expectations, we become happier, less stressed human beings.

The Wisdom to Know the Difference

Obviously, we can change some things. As a country, we endured a terrible war to banish the injustice of slavery. My namesake gave his life in that war because he believed slavery was wrong. More recently, we have witnessed remarkable change in women's freedom to be themselves. And, yes, there is sometimes room for asking for a change in behavior in relationship. However, we must never ask another to change lightly—and then only as a last resort. What we need to focus on first is how we can change ourselves.

In this context, I would remind you of the Serenity Prayer[9]:

God grant me the serenity
to accept the things I cannot change;
courage to change the things I can;
and wisdom to know the difference.

---

9 This is actually only the first part of the prayer, written by Harvard theologian Reinhold Niebuhr.

Many of us struggle fruitlessly, attempting to change things we cannot change. We thereby lose our serenity and become frustrated. I encourage you to look at your life with full awareness of what you choose to struggle with and to ask yourself whether that is how you truly wish to spend your time and energy. If you expect to change things you cannot change, you will only frustrate yourself and your partner. Sally was not going to change Ian's predilection for testing hypotheses, and Ian was not going to change Sally's wish about which attachment to use.

The trap many of us fall into in our relationships is that we don't want to accept the reality that our partner and our relationship aren't likely to change much. If only *they* would change, we think, then I'd be happy. This is another dangerous and frustrating expectation. Whether or not we are happy doesn't depend on what is outside of us but what is within. What we can most readily change is what is within ourselves.

> As Ghandi put it: "Become the change you want to see in the world."

To begin this program of change within ourselves, we can become, if we wish, more conscious of the considerable number of expectations that we burden ourselves with simply by writing them, and our reactions to having them unmet, down on paper. We can then examine them to see if we wish to keep them or release them. The next and extremely important step is to become less judgmental and more loving of ourselves and our partners by cultivating the attitude of gentle acceptance of what is.

Start with Yourself

I asked Ian and Sally to stop expecting each other to be the way they believed their partner should be and, instead, to examine their expectations of themselves, using the exercise just described. They were amazed at how many unconscious expectations they had and how distressed they became when they didn't live up to them.

Notice how often you become distressed when you don't live up to your own expectations. Become aware of the implied *should*. Then notice how you are reacting. Do you call yourself names and otherwise demean yourself? Can you, instead, practice being more loving to yourself by accepting that this is just the way you are right now?

The goal is to gradually replace stern moralistic judgment with gentle and accepting observation.

For example, today, as on many days, I started judging myself for not getting up earlier to work on this book. My inner voice sounded something like this: "You should work harder on your book or you'll never get it done. You're being lazy and indulgent. You shouldn't prioritize the cozy warmth of bed or checking your email over getting to work. Just think of how many books you could have written if you hadn't pandered to distractions."

When I noticed this judgmental mental chatter, I took a deep breath and replied, internally:

"I wish you'd stop shoulding on me, Mr. Inner Critic. Yes, I love my sleep and my cozy bed and checking my email. That's part of who I am. But don't put me down with labels like 'lazy' and 'indulgent.' I am who I am. And part of who I am is a hard worker who applies himself diligently to his writing. I will get on task when I feel ready and not before."

The internal dialog between the part of ourselves that tries to exhort us onward and upward by telling us how we should be, which I am calling Mr. Inner Critic (come up with your own name for that part in you), and the part of ourselves that says, "But I don't want to!" is basic to every human being. Our post-Puritan culture, however, has over-balanced us toward the "should" side of the ledger. We need to re-balance ourselves. Furthermore, the tone of that critical part is generally harsh and demeaning. We need to help the Inner Critic become more loving and gently encouraging rather than harshly judgmental.

Clients initially sometimes fear that by taming the Inner Critic they will devolve into inert lumps of do-nothing. I tell them that after a lifetime of pitiless self-flagellation they may well need a vacation. But we can trust that we will regain our wish to do after the vacation.

When you plant a garden, you trust that the flowers and vegetables will grow. If you saw someone standing over them shouting, "You better grow, you lazy good-for-nothings!" you would properly judge him insane. Yet we lack trust in our own capacity to grow and to be, and we are continually shouting at ourselves inside. In this way, we are truly insane.

Let Go of Trying to Control Others

Many of us will similarly try to whip our partners into line, as both Sally and Ian were doing: She to make him use the "right" attachment, he to get her to see how logical and scientific he was being. In a usually futile attempt to dispel the unhappiness born of our unfulfilled deprivation expectations, people will often try to change their partner to conform to their concept of how he or she should be. Even when your partner loves you and wants to please you, however, he or she will find it very difficult, psychologically, to accept the implied judgment of inadequacy. We want to be the apple of our loved one's eye and to be loved for who we are. A quite sane, and very stubborn, unconscious part of us will resist engaging in such an extreme makeover, as was evident in Ian's behavior.

From Sally's perspective it seemed like a small request that Ian use the proper attachment and she was understandably exasperated when he seemingly ignored her request. Her strong reaction was rooted in her history of not being valued by her father and mother. The struggle became not just to change a simple behavior but over who has the power to determine policy. That is the old parent-child struggle from childhood. Most parents believe it is their duty to teach their children the customs of the surrounding culture. When Ian's father raged at Ian for questioning the "way things are done," Ian would tune him out and do things the way he wanted behind his back—as he did with Sally, who then presented as a similar rage-aholic.

Ian said he had learned that it was "easier to ask for forgiveness than to ask for permission." That became embedded as an expectation. Gradually, he learned to break that old pattern and to discuss what he wanted to do, as in, "I'd like to try an experiment with this other attachment."

Sally gradually learned to step out of the Mommy role. When she indicated that Ian's behavior didn't meet her expectations and that he should do "better," she was taking on the parental role. Ian's inner two-year old, the one who shouts, "No, I won't!" would get triggered, though he was often unaware of it. Their interaction then became a power struggle, hidden beneath the surface, in which both of their senses of self were at stake. Few people will surrender their sense of self readily.

Yet both partners usually enter the relationship with another common expectation: That my partner will be delighted to make accommodations to please me. When they don't, or can't, we take it as evidence that they don't really love us. While nothing could be further from the truth, an incredible number of expectations begin with the false premise of "If you really loved me, you would…." When you hear yourself saying these words, inside your head or out loud, stop yourself right there.

Working with Your Expectations

Okay, so we all have expectations and we carry them into our relationships, which make our relationships and our lives more difficult than they need be. We can become more aware of what those expectations are and examine them to see if we wish to preserve them.

As we inquire into them, we can ask ourselves these questions:

1. What is it like for me to believe thoughts like this?
2. Is this thought absolutely true?
3. Who would I be if I weren't believing this?
4. What will bring me serenity?

Let's run through a specific example of how I might do this process. Take the above instance of my Inner Critic attempting to whip me to my writing desk.

What's it like for me to believe he is right?

Awful. I feel terrible. I start to believe I'm a lazy ne'r-do-well. I become discouraged and then depressed. I end up not writing at all.

Is this absolutely true?

Absolutely not. See my cogent response to him above.

Who would I be if I weren't believing this?

Well, first of all, I'd be a lot happier. I'd feel better about myself. I'd believe that I could write a good book. I'd want to make sure it got published and out in the hands of people who it would help.

What would bring me serenity?

First, I need to love myself as I am—which is sometimes lazy. But trying to whip myself into action only diminishes my serenity. So, stop whipping myself.

I encourage you to subject your own critical thoughts and expectations to such an inquiry. The process will help you decide whether these thoughts and expectations are actually helpful or harmful to you.

By doing so, you are becoming more mindful of the mental chatter that goes on within you and you are beginning to hold it up to the light of consciousness to decide whether it is in your best interests. Don't be surprised if you discover that *an enormous amount of what you think isn't helpful to you at all.*

Unconscious Expectations

While this process of inquiry is quite helpful for dealing with your conscious expectations, many of our expectations aren't conscious. How do I discover my unconscious expectations? One simple method is to observe whatever people do that you judge to be offensive, wrong, inadequate, or just plain "bad."

When I lived in Afghanistan as a boy we had a tough time trying to get the servants (all Embassy employees were required to have servants) to keep the top on the sugar bowl to keep the flies out of the sugar. My mother would gently but firmly remind them to put the top back on the sugar bowl time after time.

Finally the usually gentle and compassionate headman, Faquir, exploded one day in exasperation when my mother reminded him once more to replace the top on the sugar.

"But *memsahib*!" he said, a look of anguish on his face, "The flies eat such little sugar!"

We experienced a moment of culture shock. We were, of course, concerned about the flies spreading disease. Faquir and the other servants, lacking the concept of the microbial theory of disease, thought we were concerned about the miniscule amount of stolen sugar the flies purloined.

Exercise

I encourage you to take a moment to jot down on the left-hand third of a piece of paper a few of the things that people do or say that you find particularly offensive. In the next column list your feelings. On the third column, write down what you believe your heretofore unconscious expectation must be.

For instance, I'd write: "Leaving top off sugar." "Disgust." And then, "One should keep flies off food to forestall the spread of disease."

Because we grow up with certain expectations, we tend to accept them as "truth" rather than questioning them. That is how we become hog-tied by our culture. What we expect and even what we *see* is then deeply influenced by our acculturation. I have heard that there are two tribes in Africa living within a hundred miles of one another who have very different color perceptions. One has names for two colors in the rainbow, the other for nine. The members of the first tribe look at a rainbow and see two colors. The other tribe members see nine. Because they live so close to one another, they may have this different perception while looking at the very same rainbow. We have names for seven colors in the rainbow, though most of us actually see about five. How many do you see? How many are actually there? How do you know?

"Reality"

What is "actually there," what we so blithely assume is "reality," can become a major and often acrimonious debate in relationship. I would remind you of the story of the three baseball umpires:

The first umpire says, "I call them the way I see them."
The second umpire says, "I call them the way they are."
The third umpire says, "The way I call them makes them the way they are."

In fact, the reality on the baseball diamond, at least prior to the video review ruling, was determined by the umpire, despite fans' protests of "Yer blind, ump!" Couples often treat each other like blind umpires. But there is no place for an umpire in relationship. Couples who argue over whose reality is "better" will always have something to argue about. Do you enjoy those arguments? Would you rather be right or would you rather be happy?

Far too many people, like the second umpire, believe that the way they see reality is the way it is. They are very attached to this touching misconception. If you are such a person, please put this book down and pick up one on optical illusions.[10]

Neuroscience is teaching us that *everything* that we perceive is modulated by our prior experiences—including memories, feelings, and judgments–of similar situations. If I raise my right hand while standing behind the catcher at home plate, you might well think, "He's calling a strike." If I raise my hand in class, you probably think, "He wants to ask a question or make a comment." If you've been physically abused and I raise my hand while I'm speaking animatedly to you, you might fear I'm going to hit you.

What I would hope for you is that you will learn to step outside your expectations enough to be able to realize that, like the first umpire, we all call them the way we see them—*and that we could be wrong*. Developing this greater humility is absolutely necessary in successful relating. It's really tough to live with someone who always has to be right.

10 Or go online to <http://en. wikipedia. org/wiki/Optical_illusion.>

What Is Beautiful?

How we are acculturated determines even what we consider beautiful. Consider for a moment the different standards of feminine beauty from culture to culture. The Ubangi put plates in their lips to distend them, which to my eye is grotesque. In the painter Rubens' day, voluptuous women were considered beautiful, in contrast to our rail-thin models of today.

If you look at your local magazine rack or even the models in your local newspaper, you will find a standard of beauty that is rather unreal. First, the women pictured there tend to be severely starving. Second, many of them have been surgically enhanced. Finally, their photos are air-brushed and cunningly lighted and then cropped to present them in the best possible way. They bear little relation to real women.

But, sadly, many women assume they should look like these models to be attractive, and many men think they have been cheated if their partners don't have this look. This is an example of how we are made unhappy by unreal expectations foisted upon us by our cultural conditioning. Norman Mailer made a wry joke by saying that he was disappointed on his wedding night to discover that his wife didn't have a staple in her bellybutton, a reference to the *Playboy* foldout in the center of the magazine that many men of his day grew up on. But in fact most white women think they should look like one of those starving, surgically-augmented, and airbrushed women, and quite a few are getting piercings in their bellybuttons.

Interestingly, and probably because the vast majority of the models are white, most black women are much less invested in looking like a model and are more comfortable than their white sisters being Rubenesque. Fortunately, they have escaped laying that expectation upon themselves.

> Go back to your list of expectations. Which are unrealistic? How many are you certain are absolutely true?

The Role of Advertising and Giant Corporations

Many of our expectations have been formed by commercial advertisers, who are not much interested in our well-being. They are interested in how to get us to buy products. A primary way they do so is by manipulating us to feel anxious and inadequate so we will buy products we don't really need in order to palliate our feelings of incompleteness. We now live in a global village in which we are seen by faceless corporations primarily as consumers, as sources of cash. In the actual village of yore, where we dealt with people face-to-face, it was much harder for someone not to experience us as an actual person and therefore to care about us. Most of us care about those we interact with personally every day. It's a lot harder to care about someone who's only a credit card number. Consequently, it is no surprise that an increasing number of people feel anxious, untrusting, and believe that others are out to get them. As the bumpersnicker says, "You're not paranoid if people are really out to get you." Most large corporations are out to get our cash.

Consider, in a parallel circumstance, a medical insurance corporation. You write in to collect on your medical treatment. While the adjustor, who doesn't know you from Adam, might have some fellow feeling for your predicament, he knows that his job is to make the corporation money by turning down as many claims as he possibly can. In fact, in some such corporations, the first response is to *routinely* deny *all* first claims because, if even a small percentage of the claimants then go away, the company has made millions of dollars. If the adjustor is a person of great heart who thinks, over and again, "Gosh, this poor guy has an expensive ailment. The least I can do is to authorize some assistance," he or she will soon be looking for another job.

However, if the adjustor has grown up with you in a small town, gone to school with you and played basketball with you, and knows your kids as well as his own, he will be much less likely to deny you what you need.

Sadly, I think, we are transforming from a society of small-town caring to a society of callousness. As we do so, advertisers have been increasing our number of false expectations, such as, "If I buy this car, I will get a girl like the one who's scantily clad sitting on the hood. I will finally be loved." Or, "If I take this diet pill, I will look like the scantily clad girl, and someone will want to love me."

Deep Expectations

Some expectations are so deeply ingrained that we never even think of them as anything but the way it is. For instance, we expect to find a wonderful partner—our "soul mate"—who will make us happy. Many of the fairy tales we imbibed in childhood end up in marriage wherein, we are told, the couple lived "happily ever after." All we need do is to find the right one, our "other half," and we will be complete and completely happy.

Today's savvy couples tell me they know that's not true, that of course they'll have (minor) problems, which they'll readily settle rationally by "good communication," another widespread expectation. But they are still shocked when they find themselves with seemingly insurmountable problems, as did Ian and Sally.

When things go amiss, most people assume it's because they picked the wrong person. The antidote for that is, they assume, dumping the present partner and choosing a better model, as one would with a car that turned out to be a lemon.

Because we have grown up in a consumer culture wherein it is cheaper to replace something than to repair it, we have each had many experiences of tossing something away that's giving us a problem and shopping around for a better replacement. Why wouldn't we apply that same expectation to relationships? Especially when we're suffering within one. We therefore tend to expect that any relationship problems are the result of a poor choice of mate.

Another perspective is that a successful relationship is less about who you pick and more about the person you become inside it.

Another dangerous expectation in modern American culture is that no one should ever have to feel any pain. Got a headache? Pop this pill. Stomach upset? Take two of these. Hurting in your relationship? Get a new one. Consequently, few of us have the expectation that relationship will be hard work and that in accepting the job we have signed up for a rigorous course in psycho-spiritual development that will result in enormous soul growth if we go the distance.

I certainly didn't believe that as a young man, when I was more like a sprinter than a long distance runner. A very dear woman friend of mine gave me a card at the time, which read, in the words of Joyce Cary, a British writer:

> *Love doesn't happen like apples in Eden;*
> *it's a lot of hard, hard work.*

And while I still believe that love can blossom easily, I now know relationship is a lot of hard, hard work.

I suggest that we need to leave behind the expectation that our relationship is going to be a Happiness Factory and move on to accepting that relating is hard work that will be very painful at times. I would further suggest we reframe relationship to be a spiritual path which we undertake to journey down together. When I see my relationship not as something that should make me happy but as a challenging path that is designed to bring forth my better qualities, I can focus myself on becoming a better person. The first step in that journey is to identify and subject our expectations to the light of inquiry, letting go of as many as we can, and to turn our attention to what is real.

Harder Today?

I think relationships are much harder today than they were, for instance, just before the Civil War, and largely because of our high expectations. First of all, although few people divorced in 1860, the average marriage lasted only twelve years, largely due to early death. Second, people had fewer expectations of one another. Today we expect our partner to be a great lover, our best friend, our psychologist, an exemplary parent, a humorist, a gourmet chef, a good provider...add your own job description to the list. Back then she expected him to keep some food on the table and he expected her to cook that food and raise the kids. The gender domains were clear and separate. She didn't tell him how to plow a furrow and he didn't tell her how to bake the bread. Neither of them expected to achieve mutual orgasm every time they made love and they never had a single argument over whether the electric blanket or aspartame might cause cancer.

Certainly it made relationship easier when you knew a partner you'd grown up with since childhood in the same village. You attended the same one-room school, went to the same church or synagogue, and enjoyed the same roof-raisings and barn dances. When you decided to marry, you not only knew who your prospective mate was, you knew every other potential partner within a day's ride—and you had decided which was best for you. Your expectations were a lot closer to reality.

I hope that you are beginning to appreciate yourself and your partner for being people who are facing an enormous challenge just in dealing with both our biology and the myriad expectations that we bring to our relationships. That's not all we face. Perhaps the most important influence on the way we see the world and act in relationship is how we were raised as children.

3: THE MUMDADDY: Ghosts from the past

I have begun thinking of all relationships as
taking place between six people.
–Sigmund Freud

When we are inexplicitly drawn to another person by what we call "falling in love," part of what happens, in addition to chemistry and our expectations of how love should be, is that we are unconsciously attracted by how that person's qualities of character, good and bad, parallel those of our primary caregivers in childhood, usually Mom and Dad.

As children, our first human experience of "love" is made up of the many interactions we have with those caregivers, upon whom we are totally dependent not just for survival but for mediating our version of reality and forming our expectations. If our parents eat with chopsticks, we assume that's the right way to eat. If they teach us that love means never having to say you're sorry, we swallow that lesson whole.

These many lessons create a mosaic in our unconscious that predisposes us toward certain "types." I call this mosaic the Mumdaddy, for it is usually a composite of the qualities we perceive in Mummy and Daddy. Harville Hendricks calls it the Imago. Freud, as in the quote above, visualized my Mom and Dad standing behind you, so that I'm relating not just to you but also to them, and your Ma and Pa standing behind me, with you relating to three people as well. In short, we experience our present love relationships as powerfully influenced by those with our primary caregivers of the past, even if we aren't aware of the influence.

I use the cumbersome term "primary caregivers" because for a growing number of people it was Grandma or Uncle Charlie or foster parents rather than Mom and Dad who actually raised them. The Mumdaddy can also comprise several primary caregivers.

While any important relationship—student and teacher, employee and boss, voter and politician, athlete and coach—can contain some elements of the Mumdaddy, it is in our love relationships that we are most likely to experience the Mumdaddy most frequently and most painfully. In our love relationships we struggle to make our loved one into the perfect parent that we never actually had. While that is yet another reason love relationships are so difficult, it is also one of the principal benefits of going the distance with one person, for by doing so we have the opportunity to let go of the struggle to find a perfect Mommy or Daddy and thereby free ourselves from the sad repetition of revolving door relating.

To accomplish this transformation, however, one must be ready to let go of seeing the relationship as a happiness factory and to begin seeing it as a spiritual path. To oversimplify, we need to let go of what we think a relationship should be and begin to see what it is. What it is will include a retriggering of the issues we had with our primary caregivers. For most people, that is a difficult challenge. The temptation will be to exit the messy feelings of the relationship and find a new love with its refreshing cocktail.

A brief example

Leslie's mother didn't really want her, telling Leslie over and again that if she hadn't gotten pregnant with her (as if that was Leslie's fault) that she could have been an opera singer. She treated her daughter in some very rejecting ways. In Leslie's relationship with Dick, who seems to adore her, Leslie will often suspect that Dick doesn't really love her. A former defensive end in high school and college, Dick likes to watch college football games on Saturday afternoons during the fall season. He sees it as his relaxation after a hard week of work as a trial lawyer. An ideal Saturday for him is to sleep in, have a leisurely breakfast, do a few chores like mowing the grass or cleaning out the gutters, and then to sit down in his recliner with a cold drink and watch football. To Leslie it seems that he likes football more than her, even though on Saturday night he takes her out for dinner.

"Every other Saturday afternoon," Dick says, "she'll throw a hissy-fit because I'm watching a game rather than spending time with her."

The first thing I check on is how much quality time he is actually spending with Leslie. When they both agree that they have about *fifteen hours* of such time together each week, *which is the minimum necessary to sustain a vivid relationship*,[11] I suspect that Leslie might be getting hijacked by the Mumdaddy.

Next, I ask Dick about his experience of TV as a child.

"My dad wouldn't allow me TV time until all my homework was completed to his satisfaction. He wanted to make sure I got good enough grades to go to Stanford like him. Leslie's just like him, trying to control me."

"Well, Dick's just like my mother!" Leslie retorts.

---

11 I love Dr. Willard Harley, Jr., for coming up with this precise number. See, e.g., *His Needs, Her Needs* (1986).

They are both clearly frustrated with the situation. Leslie is relating to the ghost of her mother, who stands behind Dick's left shoulder in her psyche. Dick is relating to the ghost of his father, who stands behind Leslie's right. They have been hijacked by the Mumdaddy.

The Mumdaddy Template

Some readers will already know what I am talking about. For those who don't, or who would like a refresher course, I have adapted a few of Harville Hendricks'[12] exercises to help you experience the presence of the Mumdaddy. Let's start with a gentle trip back in the Time Travel Machine, to those thrilling days of yesteryear when you were a young child. The purpose of making such excursions back into childhood is (1) to begin to understand how much of how we relate was programmed early in our lives and (2) to choose what parts of that early program we might want to re-engineer. However, I want to forewarn you that because the Mumdaddy in each of us is a constellation of myriad old feelings, it is resistant to being changed through the mind alone. To make substantial changes in it, we will have to engage it with the heart and the feelings as well. As you enter into the following exercise, therefore, open yourself as much as you can to the feelings that come to you.

We might call this exercise "Returning to those thrilling days of yesteryear." What's the earliest house/apartment/trailer/yurt that you can remember living in? Read through the entire exercise first, or tape it so you can listen with eyes closed.

---

12 *Getting the Love You Want: A Guide for Couples* (1988).

Exercise

Make yourself comfortable and take a few deep, slow breaths. Close your eyes if you wish. Let yourself know there is nothing you have to do right now, no problem you have to solve, no place you have to go—that this is time just for you.

See your early childhood dwelling from the outside, as you approach it. Are there trees around it? Hedges? Flowers? Of what material is it made? Wood? Brick? What color is it? How do you feel as you come up to it?

Stand before the door you usually entered through. Which side is the knob/handle on? What is the door made of? Does it open inward or outward?

As you open the door, let yourself feel the temperature of the air inside. Catch the smell on the air. Slow down and take your time.

What do you see as you step inside? Hear?

Slowly walk through the dwelling, seeing what you see in each room. Use all your senses. Especially odors. What is the smell of each room?

When you come to whatever room you called "yours," even if you shared it with someone else, see the color of the walls and ceiling. What's the floor made of? Where are the windows? What's your bed look like? Do you spot a favorite toy or doll or teddy?

Lie down on your bed and feel how you feel in your room, lying on your bed.

Take your time.

When you feel done for now, get up and search through the house and garage for your caregivers. Where do you find each of them? When you find one, really look at him or her. Which clothes do they have on? See them as they were then. Look into their eyes.

Tell each of them what you really enjoyed about them and then what you found challenging about them. They will receive your observations with gratitude.

Tell them, also, what you wanted most from them and never got.

Tell each of one incident that you feel strongly about. How did you feel in that situation? Breathe into your body and watch the sensations that come up for you.

Take your time.

When you feel finished, thank each of them for listening to you. Let yourself know that you can always return to them, in this place, for further visits if you wish.

Take a few deep breaths. Gently return yourself to the present moment. Open your eyes and see the colors in the room. How do you feel now?

Take your pen and paper and jot down what came to you.

How was that for you, to go back in time? Were you able to connect with some of both painful and loving feelings from that era? The great American writer William Faulkner said, "The past is never dead. It's not even past." What we wish to do here is to become more aware of how our past interpenetrates with the present and colors it. Particularly in how it colors how we feel toward our partners. While that coloration occurs for everyone, most of us are unaware of it most of the time.

And, as the great Spanish-American philosopher George Santayana says, "Those who do not study the past are condemned to repeat it." That is very true in our love relationships, if by the word "study" we go beyond the cognitive and include feelings.

The purpose of invoking the past is not to "dredge up" painful memories. It is to become conscious of the feelings that are always present for us *but which we are usually unconscious of*. By making the unconscious conscious we can process some of its potent energy so that it loses its power over us. To process the feelings of the past, we must welcome them in, hold them before us with courage, and allow ourselves to feel them fully, as if we were the child experiencing them. What you can feel, you can heal.

Are you ready to do some work with what you discovered in your dwelling? If not, take a break until you are. The process of exploring the past takes both a courageous perseverance and a gentle loving-kindness to ourselves. You will need to go at your own speed.

When you feel ready, do the next exercise:

Exercise

Take two blank pieces of paper and draw a vertical line down the middle of each. On the left side of the first put in the heading "Pleasurable Incidents in Childhood." On the right, "How I Responded." List as many incidents—and how you responded—as you can in five or ten minutes. (You can always add items to this list later.)

For example, I would write on the left, "Cuddling with Mommy at naptime," and on the right, "Feeling warm and safe."

On the second page put the heading "Painful Incidents in Childhood" on the left and, on the right, "How I Responded." Once again list as many incidents, and how you responded to them, as you can in five or ten minutes.

For example, I would write on the left, "Dad going off to war when I was a baby," and on the right, "Not recognizing and battling him when he returned. Anger. Grief. Pain at not having a daddy present."

Place a capital E over the responses to the painful incidents. More on this later.

Some of your responses will be feelings. Others may include decisions. When my father came home after making the world safe from Hitler and interrupted my idyll with my doting mother, I decided to launch a campaign to drive him out of the house.

I would cause him as much grief as I could. I remember well the day I partially unscrewed the top on the salt shaker and he drowned his T-bone steak in salt.

Okay, let's move to the next step, which will require yet another piece of paper.

Exercise

In the top two-thirds of this piece of paper, draw a large circle, and then draw a horizontal line through the center. To one side, label the top half of the circle A and the bottom B.

Write into the top half with brief words the *positive* character traits that you found in your mother, father, and others who most impacted you as a child. Lump all the positive traits of all these people together, not distinguishing which trait came from which person. For example, I would put in both "protective" and "loving." Other words might include "warm," "creative," "intelligent," "patient."

In the bottom half, write down the *negative* character traits of the same people. I might put in "distant" and "unconscious." Once more, lump all the traits of your primary caregivers together.

It's okay to work back and forth, because seeing a negative quality might remind you of a positive one, and vice versa.

Finally, go back and <u>underline</u> the traits which you think affected you the most.

This completed circle is a treasure map that was handed to you, as a child, for choosing a partner later in life.

What We Bring to Our Relationships

You're probably wondering about that bottom third of this page. That's our next step.

> Write a capital C. After it write the words "What I wanted most as a child and didn't get was—"and complete the sentence.
> Then, write a capital D. After it write the words "As a child, I had these painful feelings over and again—"and complete that sentence.

Now for the fun part.

On yet another piece of paper, which you might title "What I Bring to My Relationship," you can bring all of this together. There are five sentences for you to complete, using the information you've assembled so far.

"What I Bring to My Relationship"

Write and then complete the following sentences:

"I have spent my life searching for a person with these character traits:" [Here list the traits from *both* A and B that you underlined within your template circle.]

"When I am with such a person, I am troubled by these traits: "[Here list the underlined traits from B, the bottom of the circle.]

"And I wish that person would give me:" [C].

"When my needs aren't met, I have these feelings:" [D].

"And I often respond this way:" [E].

At first you might find this last exercise shocking. When I do it with clients, they often show an initial resistance to accepting what seems quite obvious to me from their interactions with their partners. But sometimes we just aren't ready to see what's apparent. Nitpicking is a giveaway. One client said, "I'm not drawn by the negative traits. A negative trait my mother had was smoking. I've never dated a smoker." Next to "smoker" in her B section was "alcoholic." Every man she had dated was at least a heavy drinker.

Another objection I hear a lot is, "But when I met him I didn't *know* he was alcoholic/abusive/a pathological liar/whatever—I only found out years later." I believe you might not have known consciously. I also believe that our unconscious knows much more than we are conscious of.

Give yourself some time with it. Chew on it rather than try to swallow it whole.

The basic idea here is not a new one. The ancient Greek playwrights understood it. Freud, who'd read those dramatists, at first oversimplified the idea by pointing out that men marry their mothers and women their fathers. He also pointed out that when we find ourselves repeating the same ineffective action over and over, such as marrying yet another alcoholic, this compulsion to repeat ourselves has its roots in a mental map constructed in early childhood. He called this the repetition compulsion. So long as the map is unconscious, we will continue to repetitively seek its terrain in the present. Hopefully, these exercises will help you start to make that unconscious map conscious. Freud also pointed out that a part of us will resist becoming more conscious. Give yourself time. Chew.

Dramatizers and Avoiders

When we get hijacked by the Mumdaddy—those ghosts from our past—we will tend to behave in fairly predictable ways that we learned as children. Some people will create a drama. Others flee the scene or freeze up.

Leslie, for instance, becomes histrionic. She gets in Dick's face and shouts at him, calling him all manner of unflattering names.

Sometimes she throws a dish or a glass into the wall. Occasionally she'll threaten suicide.

Dick hunkers down inside himself. He won't say a word. Sometimes he just turns up the volume on the TV. Other times he leaves the house as quickly as he can. Sometimes he heads for the shop, where he's rehabilitating a '55 Chevy. If she follows him out there, he'll jump into his Jeep and drive around for an hour or two.

When Dick's parents fought, he'd leave the house. When Leslie's parents didn't pay attention to her, she'd throw what they called a "fit." Under pressure in the present, they each revert to the style that helped them survive childhood.

Interestingly, Dramatizers and Avoiders will tend to be attracted to each other and form a coupleship. I think they intuitively know that their partner will help balance them out. I point out to them that they each bring a positive quality to relating. Leslie has easy access to her feelings and brings the feeling component into the relationship. Once she learns how to feel through her feelings rather than dump them on Dick, she will bring a valuable component to the coupleship. Dick has the capacity to contain. He brings to the relationship a model for greater peace. Once he learns to speak up for himself, he will bring a valuable component as well.

Of course no one is totally one way or the other. Dick will sometimes blow up and Leslie can disappear. Some people are Dramatizers one day and Avoiders the next. What we're looking at here is the general tendency. Do you recognize yours? Can you accept that you have that tendency? Can you see how it helped you survive childhood? Are you open to learning more balanced ways of being?

The Least You Should Know

Here's what you might, if you wish, take from this chapter. The mind-maps we build in early childhood lead us to certain types of people to fall in love with. That process is usually outside of our awareness and includes both positive and negative character traits. Of particular interest is that we will tend to fall for those with similar *negative* character traits to those of our caregivers. Dick found a woman who rode him about watching TV just as his father had. Leslie found a man who would tune her out, just as her parents had. We will then become upset with the partner for having these negative traits, become judgmental and critical, and/or try to change him or her. *We will struggle to make them into the perfect parent we never had.* This struggle will undermine the good feelings in the relationship.

One part of your partner, wishing to please you, will try to become "a better person," i.e., the kind you think you want. Another part, however, will resist you. He or she is not consciously trying to thwart you. Resistance to control is just a healthy part of a normal human being. You cannot infringe upon another's sovereignty and expect them to be delighted in the long run.

Of course an analogous process is usually going on for the partner, who had a critical or abusive or absent parent and wishes he or she could change you into a warmly accepting lover. Then neither of you is getting what you need.

What's illuminating is to realize that we each choose a partner based upon our perception of their negatives as well as of their positives. Rather than engaging in the futile struggle to make them perfect, or at least better, we have a chance to let go of the struggle completely by accepting them as they are and ourselves as we are.

To accomplish this release, we will have to become conscious of and find ways to move through the old patterns from childhood that will erupt in our present relationship. So a positive way of framing the difficult feelings that spill into the relationship from the Mumdaddy is that you now have an opportunity to heal the wounds of the past and no longer carry them in the present.

So, when I get irked by something my partner does or says, I can *focus my attention not upon my partner but upon myself,* checking in for the Mumdaddy component. When I get a grip on that component, I have enormous leverage, because I am working on changing not another, resistant person but myself—and I have an enormous motivation to make that change.

Remember that *we are almost never angry or afraid or sad for the reason we think we are.* Most of our reactivity comes from our not seeing our partner in the present but being triggered by the shadowy figures standing behind her or him: the Mumdaddy. One of the most liberating processes that can happen in long-term relationship is that we can diminish the power that the ghosts of the past have over us in the present. Long-term relationships are guaranteed to bring those ghosts out of the closet and into the light, where we can get to know them and transform them from terrorists into mentors. That is a valuable spiritual practice. Once we let go of imagining that our partners will make us happy and grasp the idea that we can engender our own happiness by engaging in such a spiritual practice, we will then see our relationship as an accelerated learning program that will make us better, happier people.

PART II: EMERGENCY FIRST AID

Hopefully, after reading Part I, you are beginning to develop some understanding about and compassionate curiosity toward yourself and your partner. You are starting to observe your feelings, thoughts, expectations, and behavior like a cultural anthropologist from another galaxy who's fascinated by human beings. Perhaps most importantly, you are beginning to see that you are not your thoughts, most of which have been drummed into you by your culture on planet Earth. Beneath all that mental noise those thoughts can make rattling around in your head, you are really a person with deep feelings of love and compassion. Sometimes it's hard to remember that.

Once we can take a step to the side and begin observing ourselves in this way, we create a little green space in which compassion and then lovingkindness can bloom.

So you've really already taken the first and most important step you can make.

However, it's not easy for most of us to give up the painful struggle or the lonesome distance of a relationship that's running low on the chemical bliss of the Love Cocktail. We can get into some bad habits in a desperate attempt to re-ignite those loving feelings we're in love with. Or just to express our frustration that things aren't going as we expected or wished them to.

So I'm sending in a team of Emergency Management Techniques to stop the bleeding and bind up a few of the wounds so you can begin to recover. You can triage yourself and focus on what's going to be most healing for you.

Read my suggestions and choose what fits for you. What works for one couple doesn't necessarily work for another. Each coupleship, like each person within it, is unique and will need to adapt what I suggest. And, as a coupleship grows and changes through time, it will shed a skin or two. What works for you today might become obsolete tomorrow.

What I suggest that you do right away is to *stop*, *look*, and *listen*.

I further suggest that you and your partner make a pact that closes the exits for a certain period. What I ask of couples who wish to work with me is that they agree to three months of intense work on their relationship, during which time they not only will not leave the relationship but won't bring leaving up as an option. I also ask that they not be in a romantic connection with anyone else. If you are to succeed as a couple, you will need to be solely focused upon each other with both feet in the relationship and with the intent of making it work. I also tell my couples that it will probably get worse before it gets better. Be prepared for some hard work for at least a three month period. If you both know that parting during that time is not an option, it will help you do what needs to be done rather than fleeing.

Rumi has a poem that summarizes this section:

Out beyond ideas of wrongdoing and rightdoing
There is a field.
I will meet you there.

4: STOP!

All things are accomplished by not-doing.
–Lao Tze

When I was a boy growing up in a small Virginia town, the crossing at the railroad tracks had a sign that has served me well my whole life. It read, in stark black and white:

STOP! LOOK! LISTEN!

I think these are also wise rules for relating. Let's examine the first of these injunctions first.

If your relationship is in trouble—or even simply less than you wish it could be—*stop* doing what you have been doing that you *know* isn't working. Most people actually know what they are doing wrong but they keep on doing it anyway, a little more fervently each time, hoping that if they just try harder at the same strategy it will work the next time.

We all know, also, that one definition of insanity is to persist in doing the same thing even when it doesn't work. A truth that I would like to suggest is that in the realm of relationships most of us act at least a little bit insane.

Exercise

Take a moment to fetch a piece of paper and a pen or pencil. On the paper write down a one or two word description of the behaviors you continue in your relationship which you *know* are ineffective. Now, write down the behaviors your partner does that you also judge as ineffective.

Notice which list is longer. Yup, most of us are better at seeing others' faults than our own. For now, simply notice the content of both lists.

While everyone's list will vary somewhat, there will be fairly predictable behaviors on most lists that appear any time people do this exercise:

Making demands	Put-downs	Overspending
Angry outbursts	Sarcasm	Denial
Giving commands	Unilateral decisions	Lying
Playing therapist	Shoulding	Substance abuse
Withdrawal	Refusing to speak	Cheating
Tit for tat	Name-calling	Physical abuse

You know that none of these strategies is effective. They don't get us what we truly want, which is to be loved and loving.

Myron and Mimi

Myron had what is known as a sharp tongue. He often made cutting remarks. At first Mimi thought he was hilarious, so long as his rapier wit was directed toward others, but when he turned it on her she found she didn't like it much. She began retaliating, giving as good as she got, and finding that she could be pretty scathing herself. They could have been a sitcom on TV with their wicked one-liners. The trouble was that they were growing further and further apart. Finally Mimi made an appointment and dragged Myron into my office.

He indicated right away that he'd only come under duress—Mimi was threatening to divorce him. "I think couples' counseling is about as helpful as a high colonic," he said.

Though I had to admit to myself that this image was original and arresting, I simply said that I understood he was here under protest and didn't think the counseling would help.

"Well, aren't you a bright boy," he said, dripping sarcasm. I could see the problem.

"You think I'm bright because you know that I listen to you?" I asked. An often effective means of dealing with sarcasm is to reflect it literally.

"No, because you're a goddam parrot," he said.

"What you're calling parroting can be extremely helpful," I said. "But it seems to me that the real issue here is that your wife is ready to leave you. Is that what you want to happen?"

"It's up to her. The door's right there."

"Is that what you want to happen?"

He put his head down for a moment, then finally shook it.

"No," he said.

"You'd like to maintain the relationship."

"If possible."

I told them that it was quite possible, but that they'd both need to stop dishing out the "funny" put-downs. Each was prioritizing "humor" over the partner's feelings—which were being hurt by the barbs directed at them. When they got hurt, they pulled away, creating distance. I told them that their Love Bank was going into the red.

"What the heck's the Love Bank?" Myron asked.

I said that I was glad that he'd asked.

The Love Bank

For over thirty years I have been talking to my clients about what I call the Love Bank. Imagine my delight when I found, in the very helpful work of Dr. Willard Harley, Jr., the same name for the same concept.[13] I am only slightly put out that Dr. Harley beat me to publication. I am honored to find another couples' therapist who thinks along parallel lines. Here's the idea:

Each of us carries within a portion of the brain an accounting system that adds positive emotional credits when our partner does something we like and subtracts them when he or she does something we don't like. In the beginning of a relationship, when we're high on the Love Cocktail, massive credits get deposited in the Love Bank. But then we have that first disillusionment, when one partner has a meltdown or when we're hurt that the anniversary is forgotten. Withdrawals, small at first, begin to bleed out of the account.

Myron's witticisms were hurtful to Mimi. Her first strategy—to give it back to him in kind—only made the matter worse. The Love Bank was bleeding out. Wisely, Mimi recognized this and told him they needed to change the way they spoke to each other.

---

13 See, for instance, *His Needs, Her Needs: Building an Affair-Proof Marriage* (1986).

As we begin manifesting the ineffective behaviors listed above, we make larger and larger withdrawals from the deposits on hand, until finally we're into the red—and we start seeing red. Every little thing our partner does now irritates us, and we find ourselves becoming someone we wouldn't have recognized a short time before. We assume we've "fallen out of love."

Without a daily infusion of positive credits, a relationship will wither. Yet most of us, perhaps accustomed to the ease with which we accumulated love credits during the Love Cocktail stage, tend to neglect our relationship's needs and turn it over to a kind of autopilot, expecting that it will be fine on its own. We turn our attention to other things, such as work or kids or golf. We expect a partner to shrug off our barbed wit. One day we awake with a shock to realize that our bank account has been bleeding dry.

What then usually happens is an old, sad story. We meet someone new, or start having strong feelings for an old friend. Yup, Ma Nature is doing her thing. We feel the old electricity with this other person. We find ourselves making excuses to spend time together, to talk intimately rather than "wittily"—and soon we find ourselves in love with someone who's not our partner.

Well, what did you expect? You've met this attractive new person at work or the grocery store and find that it's really easy to talk, that you understand each other...While at home there are angry outbursts and critical judgment and demands and put-downs and diapers to wash.

It's not a level playing field.

The old relationship is deep into the red, while the new one is quickly amassing credits in the black. And we wonder why the divorce rate is so high.

If you're already beginning a new relationship, stop it and get yourself to a good affair-recovery counselor immediately. You will need professional help. 90% of relationships that get it can be saved.

If like Mimi you are simply aware that the Love Bank is running low on or totally out of credits, you must turn around the negative cash flow into a positive one. The very first action you must take is to *stop doing whatever it is that you are currently doing that is depleting the Love Bank.*

In Mimi and Myron's case that meant placing a moratorium on any humor that had as its target the other partner. I suggested that they make themselves the butt of any witticism and gave them a few examples from Mark Twain. For example, "I don't know why people have so much trouble giving up smoking. I've done it hundreds of times."

But what if I don't know what I'm doing wrong?

First, I would suggest that when you find yourself using a word like "wrong" that you substitute a word like "ineffective." This practice will help shift you from a judgmental, moralistic perspective to a more practical one—and make the changes you wish to make easier to make.

If you really don't believe you know what you're doing that isn't effective, you can always ask your partner and your more honest friends the following question:

"What do I do or say that most annoys you or makes you want to resist me?"

How do you feel when you hear the answers? Hurt? Angry? Scared that you aren't as "cool" as you thought you were? Do you want to *deny* that these responses might be true?

Are you more attached to your *image* of who you are than to who you might actually be? Is that tough for you to deal with? Would you rather deny reality and stay with your comforting *delusions*?

A single man whom I'll call Mike came to see me because he was puzzled why women tended to turn off to him. He was nearly fifty and had never been married. He was relatively attractive and quite fit, being an ardent cyclist. When I shook hands with him I could detect no offensive body or mouth odors. He had an engaging smile.

"Recent example," he said. "Just had a date set up by an Internet company. We're theoretically compatible. She's a psychiatrist, very bright woman. We're chatting over coffee and she jumps up from the table and says, 'I'm insulted!' I have no idea what I said or did that she found insulting. Told her I had no intention of insulting her and that if I'd just wanted to insult her I could have done that when we talked on the phone without having to make a two hour drive. She calmed down. But I never want to see her again."

"And you have no idea what she found insulting."

"Nope. This kind of thing happens all the time. Another time...."

He gave me two more examples. While he had attempted to "smooth it over" in each case, as he had done with the psychiatrist, the incipient relationships ended.

"Women are just nuts!" he said, with considerable fervor. I suspected that might be a clue to his problem and began asking him about his mother, who he portrayed as pretty crazy, and his sister, who abused him physically.

I also pointed out to Mike that he himself had come up with a brilliant question for such situations: "What did I say or do that offended you?" I suggested that, rather than attempting to smooth things over, he ask that question when he was in such a situation again. I had the suspicion that an honest woman might say something like, "You just made a derogatory generalization about all women. I hate it when people do that. I need to have you see me as an individual, not as a member of some group."

As we began to explore the problem, we discovered that he is carrying a lot of unexpressed anger at women that is rooted in his experience of his mother and his sister. He was unaware of how this anger would suddenly flash out, frightening women away. He truly wanted a loving connection with a good woman but his old anger kept contaminating his potential relationships. He had to face the discrepancy between the way he saw himself, Mr. Nice Guy, and the way many women saw him—a man who hated women.

To some extent or other, every human being on the planet has to deal with this difficult contradiction between who we'd like to think we are and who we actually are, between the False Self and the Real Self. One of our most important jobs in life is to make the journey from the False to the Real, and sometimes it takes a lifetime.

Relationships have a way of bringing us face-to-face with our Real Selves. And, as we become realer ourselves, we become candidates for a Real Relationship. A step we can take in that direction is to ask friends and lovers, "What did I just do or say that upset you?"

But what if I find I can't stop my ineffective behavior?

When you identify what it is that you are doing that is ineffective, you can then move on to not-doing. The capacity to stop acting ineffectively sounds easy, but it isn't for most of us. Over a lifetime we develop some bad habits. Like most of us, you probably grew up in a family that threw them around like confetti. It's the norm. Then you fell in love and imagined they'd all evaporated. The Love Cocktail stage demonstrates to us that our bad habits can be fended off. But now here they are again, only worse! Old habits are hard habits to break. To help break them, keep track—on paper.

Start with your top three. Write down each time you do one. Put in the date and time. Then ask yourself what might have been a more effective strategy, and write that down as well. For instance, imagine that you have identified in yourself the common pattern of attempting to be helpful by telling your partner what he or she should do. Let's say you are feeling awful that your partner hasn't called his mother to thank her for her generous Christmas present. You find yourself trying to get him to do what you think is right:

"You should call your mother to thank her for the Lexus."
"That's hard for me."
"You can't dial a phone number?"

Occurrence	Ineffective Behavior (Type)	More Effective
25 August, 10:32 a.m.	"You should call Mom." (Shoulding)	"I wish you'd call Mom."
25 Aug 10:33 a.m.	"You can't dial a phone number?" (Sarcasm)	"I really wish you'd call."

Please be prepared to be horrified at how often you indulge in ineffective behavior. Do not beat yourself up for doing so. Don't put yourself down or call yourself names. Apply the same principles of compassion to yourself as would like to apply to your partner. You are developing compassionate loving-kindness for yourself, too.

When you train a puppy to stop peeing wherever he wants and to only go in the box with the old newspaper in it, you simply keep putting him back on the paper when he makes those having-to-go signs. Similarly, you are training yourself to become mindful of when you lapse into ineffective patterns. Just keep putting yourself back on the paper of effective action. And, as you give the puppy a Milk Bone when he does it right, reward yourself for your successes. Tell yourself, "Good job!" or buy yourself an ice cream.

Psychologists, and dog trainers, know that rewards are much more effective in helping to change behavior than punishments. Actually, punishments can thwart the process.

Shout, shout, get it all out

So you're working at not-doing what's ineffective. What do you do instead?

Much of the time you will simply zip your lip and observe your inner process. This small change is profound. First, you halt the ineffective behaviors, what psychologists call "acting out." Instead, you are *observing in*. Simply watch your inner process. It helps many people to imagine that they are scuba diving deep in a cool blue ocean. Down here it is quiet, except for your breathing through the regulator, and very still. Up on the surface of the ocean there are waves, maybe even a hurricane, whatever is happening outside. It's a long way off. You are watching it as if from a great distance, safe from the turbulence above.

Not-doing will raise your frustration level at first. When you get frustrated enough, say to those present, "I going to do some chaotic meditation," go into the bedroom, close the door, lie down on your back on the bed and hit the bed with open palms while screaming your head off. Shout, shout, get it all out, as Tears for Fears sings.

Just don't do it in your partner's face. That's the angry outburst that will usually injure a relationship. By dumping your frustration separately, you (1) take care of yourself by burning off your adrenaline while (2) sparing your partner the torrent. He or she will appreciate it. It's probably a good idea to forewarn him or her (and the kids) of what you'll be doing so they have a context. For example, you can say:

> "I don't want to indulge in angry outbursts at you or the kids any more. When I'm frustrated and angry I'm going to go into the bedroom and dump my anger there in chaotic meditation, not on you."

After you've gotten it all out, take a few deep breaths. Is it really all cleared? If not, go back at it. Stick with it until you've drained the adrenaline. I find that I need to go through my feelings at least three times. Keep asking yourself, "When have I felt this way before?" and be open to past feelings piggybacking onto the present. Welcome your ghosts. I suggest you assume that you are never angry (or sad or afraid) for the reason you think you are. When we follow a feeling, we usually discover yet other situations and images flashing up into consciousness in the wake of the triggering one. Often one domino knocks over a whole line of them. We'll discuss this process in more detail in Chapter 8. For right now I want you to do what you can with it. Do not squelch your feelings; they will only grow more intense in the dark. Just don't dump them on your partner.

When you've really flushed the feelings, not just at this present situation but at all the similar ones you can remember, you'll feel cleansed and clear. Only now ask yourself, "Is there anything, that's specific and doable, that I wish right now?"

Often, getting your anger out will in itself take care of the problem. If you still have a wish ("That you call Mom."), you'll be able to ask for it in a civil tone. Practice in the bedroom. Look in the mirror. Can't hit that civil note? See that angry look on your face? The furrowed brow? More anger needs to come out first.

Note the underlying truths here:

1. People *will* get mad at each other in relationships. That's normal.
2. Instead of dumping your anger on your partner or swallowing it, burn the adrenaline.
3. Stay with it until you discover the old childhood wound beneath the feeling.
4. Come back to your partner civilly, and ask for what you want, if you have a specific and doable wish. Ask for 100% of what you want and be prepared to not get what you want much of the time.
5. If your partner doesn't wish to meet your request, accept that and find a way to organize around that reality. Do not expect your partner to meet all your wishes. If you get mad about his or her non-compliance, return to your scream room.

I'm using the example of frustration because that's what will probably come up when you are working on containing your dumping of irritation on your partner. But you might find that sadness wells up when you realize how far your relationship has drifted from those early days of bliss. Or you might feel scared of how big the feelings are within you. Go through the same steps with any feeling that comes up for you. What I'm suggesting you do is to STOP doing those things that you know are ineffective and START building in a pressure relief valve so you're neither holding feelings in nor flying off the handle at your partner. We need to treat our partners at least as well as we do our friends. Are you doing that now?

Ask for 100% of what you want

On #4 above, I can hear some gasps. "Ask for *everything* I want?" Sure. Why not? The worst thing that can happen is you won't get what you're asking for—which is exactly what will happen if you don't ask. *Stop* holding yourself back. The alternative is to have an internal debate that goes something like the one Leslie described going on within when she's washing dishes and Dick's still glued to the tube:

> *"I really wish he'd help with the dishes tonight."*
> *"But he hates to do dishes."*
> *"Well, I've had a really hard day and I cooked a great dinner and..."*
> *"He's just gonna get grouchy if you ask him."*
> *"Yeah, and he ought to just offer. Can't he see that I'm exhausted?"*
> *"Nope. He's gonna watch football. He's just a selfish twit."*

And so on. Pretty soon the debater has worked herself up into a rage that probably includes incidents of man's unfairness to woman over the past 5000 years. He's lucky if she doesn't bean him with the iron skillet.

I use a woman in this example. Although both sexes are certainly guilty of such withholding, our society is (still) much harder on women in teaching them to ask not what others can do for them but what they can do for others. They are "supposed" to be the nurturers and caretakers. Consequently, it's harder for most women than for most men to (1) realize they'd like something and (2) ask for it. Having said that, I would add that there are plenty of men with the same difficulty.

Examine yourself and ask, "Am I asking for 100% of what I want? Do I understand that I can't always get what I want? Can I gracefully accept a 'No'? Or do I fall into a kind of trance or paralysis around even letting *myself* know what I'd like?"

A paralyzing old feeling

Jill and Jessica came into my office looking glum, as many couples do at first. They sat at opposite ends of the couch with their arms crossed over their hearts as if to protect them from further injury.

"She just won't meet my needs," Jill said.

"You won't tell me what you need," Jessica said.

"Well, if you loved me you'd know what I needed," Jill countered.

Many people get stuck with an old feeling on this issue. It's a good example of how the past has not passed but is still with us in the present. When we were infants, we couldn't ask with words for what we needed—though our lives depended on receiving it. The best we could do was kick and squall. Our caretakers had to read our cries and movements and decide what to do for us. To the extent that they could read our signals accurately and were patiently-loving in their caretaking, our needs were met. When a feeling parent observes what his child is attempting to communicate, he can empathize. The mirror neurons in his brain and heart resonate with those of his child and he knows what his child needs. Sadly, most caretakers were too tired or too anxious or too needy themselves to be able to be very good at reading us and responding appropriately, so most of us didn't get our needs met. Unmet childhood needs leave us with an underlying anxiety and frustration that will be retriggered in our adult relationships. The neglected child still lives on in the adult and hopes that this time, in this relationship, his or her needs will be met—*beginning with the primary, life-giving need to be attended to without having to ask.*

I can't tell you how often I've heard some permutation of the phrase "She/he ought to know what I need without me having to ask for it!" in my consulting room. Many people want to be given to without having to make their wishes clear. They expect their partners to be psychic. When the partners inevitably fail, sooner or later, the non-asker then tends to feel an upwelling of feelings such as an infant might display when he or she has had to wait to be fed long past the point of hunger.

The logical antidote for this issue, of course, is to not expect your partner to be a mind-reader and to push yourself to ask for what you want. But we are not ruled solely by logic. Understand that you might well have a huge emotional resistance to asking. While we can understand this concept, a big part of many of us still longs to finally receive the empathic nurturing that we lacked in childhood. You will probably have to feel through that old pain to free yourself to ask in the present.

The sad truth is that even if we have a perfect partner in the present who can anticipate our every need and meet it for us, even that won't fill the hole in the soul from the past wounds of having had unmet needs. We must face the reality of our archaic wounds and grieve that we didn't have perfect caregivers. When we grieve enough, we come at last to acceptance of what is. When we can do so, we stop struggling to make our partner perfect and allow him or her to be who they are. We will then stop projecting our anger at our caregivers onto our partners. We can then ask for what we want on the off chance that we might get it.

I strongly suggest that you stop yourself from stopping yourself asking for what you want.

The problem of "No!"

As if that's not enough, yet another problem tends to shadow this one. After we grasp this concept of asking for what we want and push ourselves to make a request, what happens when we get a "No"?

"I hardly ever ask for anything and when I finally do, you won't do it!" Jill shouts.

For Jill, all her prior withholding has created a sense of *entitlement*—she thinks that because she didn't ask for much Jessica should always give what she does ask for. "Because I ask for so little, you should know that and then give me the few crumbs I do ask for," is her misguided logic.

Being trapped by a sense of entitlement is another reason to ask for 100% of what you want. If you are asking for everything you want, your partner will also know how much you aren't getting and you won't have any withheld wishes that are causing you resentment.

But the main problem with not having your needs met is archaic, a constellation of old feelings from infancy. The old rage from not having been given to is likely to be triggered. Some people will explode in a fury that shocks even them. That would be the Dramatizer. Others implode and say, aloud or to themselves, "That's it! I'm never going to ask for another thing from you as long as I live!" That's the Avoider. Others just reach for their drug of choice or go shopping or gambling to numb out.

I hope that you are beginning to get a sense of how much of what we believe is going on in the present in our relationship is actually the lingering echoes of archaic wounds from the past that are getting retriggered by the very love and hope that the new relationship holds out. It's as if the archaic wounds, which have often been deeply frozen for years, can sense the warm love that's in the relationship and crawl out of their dark deep freezer toward the light and warmth in the hopes of being thawed and healed. Our job is not to attempt to slam the freezer door on them but to welcome them and heal them.

They can be healed, but not by infinite giving from a perfect parent-surrogate.

An Attitude Adjustment

Of course most of us prefer a blissful, soul-throbbing relationship. But no relationship will be that way every day after the Love Cocktail wears off. What we can do is to stop looking at relationship as what we think it should be and to begin looking at it as a pathway toward the growth of soul and the healing of old wounds. Who do you want to stop being and who would you like to become? Instead of staying stuck in the old patterns, you now have the opportunity to grow both your relationship and yourself. We are able to change and grow at any age, if we really wish to do so.

Is this path of psycho-spiritual development a hard one?

You bet it is. Real relationship is not for the faint of heart. You will become discouraged when, for instance, you're trying to stop some ineffective behavior and it just won't go away. It took Mimi and Myron over six months to quell their hurtful witticisms. When that happens, don't beat yourself up. Remind yourself that to err is human. Then ask for help in making the change. That's what we therapists are for.

Finally, I'd suggest that you emulate Socrates. When his wife Xantippe got enraged with him that he preferred philosophizing with his students to accumulating drachmas in the market so she could buy some new finery, she picked up the chamberpot and, in front of his stunned students, and dumped it over his bald pate.

The wisest man in Athens mildly wiped away some of the offal from his bushy white eyebrows and said to his class, "That's my wife Xantippe. It is from her that I have learned the virtue of forbearance."

What a guy. His example holds up an ideal toward which we can grow.

Summary: *Stop* doing what you know isn't effective in relating. Instead, feel your feelings away from your partner. Ask for 100% of what you want, and be prepared to hear "no." Become just like Socrates.

5: LOOK!

Why do you observe the splinter in your brother's eye
and never notice the plank in your own?
–Jesus

It is helpful in relating to look at our partners, and ourselves, with as much compassion as possible.

People aren't all the same. Some of our differences are genetic.

When Yashi and I got married over 20 years ago, I told her I didn't like Brussels sprouts.

"You haven't had them the way I make them," she said, aptly confident in her culinary skills.

I agreed to try them once again. They still tasted horrible to me.

Yashi was hurt. She kept trying to make them differently. She put in more butter and less salt. I kept telling her it wasn't her cooking but my taste buds.

Finally our son Nate brought home from biology class two little white strips of paper. He handed one to Yashi and asked her to taste it. She flicked a dainty tongue tip on the paper.

"This is just paper," she said. "It's tasteless."

When I put the other piece on my tongue, I quickly spat it out, yelling "Yuck!"

Nate explained that both pieces of paper contained a chemical called phenylthiocarbamide which is also in Brussels sprouts. Some people can taste it and others can't, depending upon their genes.

Thanks to Nate, Yashi hasn't tried to get me to eat Brussels sprouts since.

I love to use these little slips of PTC paper in couples' groups because it so unequivocally establishes the fact that people are different.

Lacking this kind of information, people will tend to assume that others, and particularly loved ones, must be similar to themselves. There is a part of us that wants this to be true and in that first, Romantic stage, we are most aware of how similar we are. The taste test shows vividly that we are in fact different biologically, to say nothing of the differences that we take on through our varied upbringings.

The moral of this story is that we need to see who our partners really are, not who we assume or wish they are.

While we might know our partners in some ways, in others we will be wildly wrong.

We need to continually readjust the way we see things. We usually begin relating with rose-colored glasses and then trade the rosies in for some very dark ones. The switch tends to be proportional. That is, to the extent that we once saw the partner as angelic we now see him or her as devilish.

To most of us it seems our partners have many foibles whilst we have but a few. (Remember the exercise at the beginning of the last chapter? Were you one of the few who can see more of the planks in your own eye? Good for you! Or are you overly critical of yourself?)

Most of us assume that we have fewer foibles than our partners because we are better than them. This is a wicked game the ego plays called "Aren't I Wonderful (Compared to You)!"

There are some people who do precisely the opposite, seeing themselves as awful and their partners as most excellent. Either perspective is based upon skewed vision.

People tend to pick partners who are roughly at their same level of psychospiritual development. As my good friend Dr. Stephen Khamsi puts it: "Who you're with is where you're at."[14] The foibles that we see in them are likely to be mirrors of those in ourselves.

But My Partner is Really Evil

Most of the people I have known over a lifetime are basically good, decent folks. However, I will grant that there are a few bad apples out and about. Recently, we've heard a lot about what some priests have been doing to the children in their care. There are also stone cold killers. One of my woman clients discovered, only after he was arrested after many years of marriage, that the serial rapist in their city was her husband. She had had no clue.

As we move from the rosy glasses stage to the dark glasses, we can begin to build a case that our partner is one of the badies. And then torture ourselves with whether we should stay in the relationship.

Well, let's take a good look at the facts of who you're with. The facts, not your dark imaginings.

What most marriage counselors tell their clients is that there are three reasons to leave a relationship, at least temporarily: Addiction, Adultery, and (Physical) Abuse.

In each case, you might well need to say either, "I'm done" or "I can't live with you until you stop this behavior for at least six months. I hope you will get serious help and be able to change. After six months, I will want you to give me a release to talk to

14 Stephen says he got this from Karen Sexton. Thank you, Karen!

your therapist/rehabilitation center and I'll decide at that point whether to give it another go."

In addition to the three A's, each of us will probably have a few other bottom-liners. For instance, many people would shun someone who is chronically suicidal. Similarly, most of us would find it difficult to live with a chronic liar or someone who is so self-centered that they have no capacity to empathize with anyone else. Or, quite possibly, a serial killer. What's your bottom line?

If you are confused about where this line is for you, figure it out with a good therapist. If it really drives you bananas that he votes Republican and you find you can't change yourself in a reasonable time, you might need to say to your partner, "I know this is my problem, but I really can't be together with someone who votes Republican. If you can't change parties for me, I'm afraid we'll have to split up."

You think I'm joking? It's happened. If it's a bottom-liner for you, that's reality. From the other perspective, it might not be a bottom-liner for you that your partner is a serial killer. You might decide, as some people do, that you like a relationship with someone who's in prison.

Ask yourself Dear Abby's question: "Am I better off with or without him/her?" It's a practical question, not a cosmic one. The answer will vary from person to person.

Once you have answered the question, let go of it. If you've decided to be with this partner, warts and all, then see their foibles not as something to correct but as part of the package deal that you are choosing to take on. Rather than focusing on how "bad" our partner is, focus on what they do and say that you like. A psychological truth is that what we look for we will tend to find.

I suggest to my clients that they make a practice of catching each other doing things they like and telling each other what they are. I call these *warm fuzzies*. I tell couples to come up with at least five warm fuzzies a day per person. This simple exercise has turned around many a relationship. As they look for one thing to say "I like it when you..." to, they find many more there. When they say what they like, they feel better—and their partner is more likely to continue that positive behavior. They co-create a magical upward spiral.

Warm fuzzies v. cold pricklies

What was your early experience in your family of origin of the proportion of warm fuzzies (positives) to cold pricklies (negatives)? Does that relate to which vernacular you tend to use in your relationship? Which do *you* like to receive?

Psychologists who study such things have come up with a very precise formula: In a relationship, when the ratio of warm fuzzies to cold pricklies falls below 5:1, divorce is imminent. One of these researchers[15] claims that he can tell within a few minutes of observing a couple whether they will divorce—with over 90% accuracy—simply by watching for such cold pricklies as criticism, contempt, defensiveness, stonewalling, and a lack of repair attempts.

We all actually have a sense of the truth of this formula. When we see another couple who are speaking positively toward each other, we figure they are doing well. And vice versa.

Watch what you say to your partner (and how you say it). If your tone and language is critical and demanding, or loaded with sarcasm and contempt like Myron and Mimi's, I advise you to clean up your act if you want this relationship to last. As we stressed in the last chapter, look at what you're doing and stop doing it.

Substitute warm fuzzies. Look for what your partner is doing *that you like* rather than what they are doing that you hate. Tell them what you see, beginning the sentence with "I like...." For

---

15 John Gottman and Nan Silver, *The Seven Principles for Making Marriage Work* (1999) pp. 39-40.

example: "I like it when you bring me a cup of coffee." "I really like the way you kiss me." "I love it when you rub my neck after a long day." Keep it positive. Don't say, "I like it that you haven't verbally abused me this week." Instead say "I like the way you're speaking to me this week." And don't just limit yourself to words: A warm smile, a big hug, a tender touch all count as positives.

When we begin looking for what we like, we see more of it.

Remember, you'll need to do at least five a day, on the off chance that you'll slip up once with a cold prickly out of habit. When you do go prickly, which we all do occasionally, catch yourself, apologize, and start on a new count of five more warm fuzzies.

The Inner Critic

In addition to watching our language and tone, we can also profit enormously from observing our internal critic. This is that part of us who judges and blames. Some people are harder on themselves, other people are harder on others, and yet others tear into everybody.

Begin noticing the voice of the Inner Critic (IC) inside you. It will often sound like one of your parents. "How could I have been so stupid!" "Golly, that person is really dumb." "I hate the way she dresses!" "I am too fat."

Catch yourself, take a deep breath, and report the observation to yourself without condemning yourself. You can simply say, inside, "criticizing, criticizing." Take another deep breath and substitute a warm fuzzy: "I am well-insulated for the winter." "She has a very original fashion sense."

This technique, which is called *cognitive substitution*, works for some people quite effectively. You simply need to watch for the IC and replace his (or her) cold prickly with a warm fuzzy—relentlessly but without beating yourself up. Just the process of watching your mind at work as if from a distance can be enormously helpful. You are separate from your IC. You are not the IC.

Exercise

Now take this process a step deeper. Whose voice does your IC's remind you of? How did you feel when that person derided you with that tone of voice? Find a quiet, private place for yourself and take a few breaths. Go back in time and tell that person how you feel about it and what you see it did to you. It is *not* necessary or important to speak to the actual person; in fact, it can complicate your process. This process is not about punishing others; it's about freeing yourself from the burdens of the past.

As we were done to, so we now tend to do to ourselves and to our loved ones. You have an opportunity to break this negative cycle. Look for it in yourself honestly and begin to make the change.

Projection

Try this: Go to a coffee shop and watch a total stranger for a few minutes. What kind of person do you think they are? Who do they remind you of? Take a piece of paper and jot down the story that you make up about them.

We've all had this experience. We see a beautiful person and imagine them to be trustworthy loyal helpful friendly courteous kind obedient cheerful thrifty brave clean and reverent. When they speak—or pull out a gun to rob the barista—we might be disillusioned, to put it mildly.

You may have had the opposite experience of seeing someone who reminded you of Attila the Hun and scared the daylights out of you. Getting to know him, you discovered that he was a very kind man who is caring for his invalided mother. Attila the Honey.

What we have done in either case is to project our fantasy onto the other person as a movie is projected onto a screen. Sometimes we may even be right to some extent, if we stay general enough. But ultimately our fantasies have much more to do with us than with who the other actually is.

We begin our relationships like two strangers meeting on a train, each lugging a suitcase. We're attracted to something in the other (which is probably driven by our Mumdaddy and biochemistry), sit down across from one another, open our suitcases—which contain all of our past experiences, good and bad, of former relationships—and begin selecting these articles to toss upon our partners. I imagine she's musical and toss onto her shoulder the playbill from the concert I attended in Vienna. She imagines I'm athletic and tosses onto my head her gym shorts from high school PE. Soon each of us is covered by the old clothing and artifacts of the other's baggage. Perhaps you can still see one actual eye peeking out. We decide we know the other. After all, they certainly look a lot like all we've known and met.

This process, which psychologists call projection, happens to all of us all the time. The human brain is uncomfortable with excessive novelty and likes to pigeonhole new people into old formats. With our romantic partners, we are much more likely to project than with anyone else. We must become aware that we project, and seek to undo some of our most egregious projections, if we are to truly see what *is* rather than continually watch a movie that we create.

How can we do so? First, accept that most of what you think you see is probably not real, *especially with regard to your partner*. Scary, isn't it? If we can't trust our eyes, what can we trust? Remember that to the human eye the world looks flatish and the sun appears to rotate about us, two "truths" that people believed and the Catholic Church rather brutally insisted upon for many generations. We now know, of course, that neither of these apparent truths is true.

We also know that this book in your hands is composed of trillions of quickly moving atoms and an enormous amount of space—neither of which can you see.

"But I know my partner!" you insist. Well, I'll grant that you know him or her in some ways. But in others you don't. Because of the intense feelings that relationships swim in like fish in water, many of them old feelings from childhood, we project enormously in them. We *see* in our partner much of what we experienced as young children with our primary caregivers. They were our first experience of a loving relationship and we take our feelings around that into our present relating. Go back to the Mumdaddy exercise and remind yourself of this reality.

• • •

We can never know our partners completely. When we think we do we are fooling ourselves, with the result that we take them for granted and become bored. Instead, try on the idea that much of who you *think* your partner to be is actually a projection of your own mind and that he or she is actually an infinite mystery that you can continue to explore for at least a lifetime. Resist the all too human urge to see your partner's soul as a child's wading pool rather than the deep and muddy Mississippi. You'll find the latter perspective a lot more interesting.

How can we drop our rose- or pitch-colored glasses and really *see* our partners? One thing I suggest you do as a couple is to take a test. By "test" I mean what psychologists, who sometimes torture the language, like to call "instruments for measurement of psychological tendencies." Please hear that any such "instruments" are fairly crude. The will not pin you to the wall like a butterfly. What they can sometimes do is to give you more understanding of yourself and your partner. I encourage you to approach them in the spirit of fun, with an open curiosity. Take what they say that is helpful to you and discard the rest.

Take a Test

When couples come into my office, sometimes entrenched in their beliefs that they know exactly who their partner is, I encourage them to take a personality test such as the Myers-Briggs, the 16 PF, or an Enneagram instrument. This exercise can serve two purposes: It can show how similar or different the two individuals actually are, and it can demonstrate that someone's personality is fairly deep-seated and therefore unlikely to be changed by the partner's best efforts. What often happens is that each partner becomes more understanding of and less inclined to try to change their partner.

If you have never taken such a test, it can be an enjoyable and enriching experience. A simple way to do so is to buy a copy of *Please Understand Me*, which contains an abbreviated form of the Myers-Briggs and a clear explanation of what your personality type and that of your partner's is and how the two might interact. The authors stress two important points: (1) Our personality types are relatively immutable. (2) None are totally good or bad; they simply are. Consequently, why not accept the person you love for who he or she is and enjoy getting to know someone who is different from you.

A fascinating tendency of human beings is to fall in love with someone who is *not* the same personality type. The catchy aphorism for this tendency is: "Opposites attract." Actually, that aphorism overstates the case. Usually, opposites don't attract. What we find attractive is an interesting study, but one vector is certainly someone who's somewhat similar but not *too* similar to us. One would think life might be easier with someone who's just like ourselves. But in fact some part of us likes the differences that we then love to complain about.

So Spenders and Savers fall in love, as do Felixes and Oscars, Hermits and Party Animals, Avoiders and Dramatizers, Thinkers and Feelers—you can add your own wisdom of the dialectic to the list. Once they get together, partners then tend to polarize further, to fight about these differences, and to struggle to get the partner to be more like themselves and some infinitely loving parent.

This is a futile struggle. Give it up. Who you're with is where you're at. Let go of your projections and fantasies and begin dealing with what is.

Once you understand that most of us fall for someone with at least some differences from ourselves, you can accept and even relish the differences as points of learning rather than trying to make your partner into your image.

Jocko and Victoria

I remember fondly a very unlikely couple. A stunning former debutante, a waif-like Aubrey Hepburn look-alike, fell for a hulking, tattooed biker. On the surface they seemed to be extreme opposites. For a few years she traded in her gowns for leather chaps and roamed the roads on the back of his Harley. Then she got pregnant and started making some demands: That he marry her, lock down a steady job, scrub the tattoos, cut his long hair, sell his Harley and buy a Volvo station wagon. When he rebelled at this last step, she dragged him in for counseling. He sat and glowered, doing his

Marlon Brando impersonation from *The Wild One*. She pointed out that he had responsibilities now. While readily agreeing, I pointed out that she was trying for an extreme makeover of the man she'd fallen in love with. She decided to see another therapist.

Two years later Jocko came in by himself. He said he'd accommodated to everything she'd asked of him because his daughter, now almost two, was so important to him. Yes, he'd even gone through the painful process of having several tattoos deleted. But after the birth their sex life had stopped. His wife had told him that she didn't understand it, but she was no longer turned on by him. She thought they should divorce. He was crushed, and angry.

I pointed out that she'd been sexually attracted to a Wild One and had then set about to transform him into the kind of man she'd be so bored with at the debutante balls.

He sat as if stunned, then nodded slowly.

"Man, you are so right," he growled.

He left his steady job at Safeway, went back to work as an independent mechanic, got his bike out of hock (he'd lied about selling it), and let his hair grow again. His wife threw a fit, kicked him out of the house her daddy had purchased for them, and left me a nasty message on my voicemail, which I didn't bother to return.

Six months later, he dropped by to thank me. They'd gotten back together and their sex life was "groovy" again. She accepted that he was a biker mechanic. He accepted the Volvo and the rather stiff functions with her family. (Her mother kept dragging him aside and pestering him for a bag of weed, which he staunchly denied ever using.) They were saving up to buy a sidecar for the baby.

"I sold me down the river, man," he said. "When I got me back, she fell for me all over again. I'd heard marriage was about give and take. Ours was me giving and her taking. But what she really wanted was a man who could say No to her sometimes."

"Sounds like the relationship is more balanced now," I said.

He was silent for a long moment.

"It's two people now," he said. "Now that I'm not a clone."

Yup. That's what long-term relationship is about. Two people. Being who they are while being willing to accept the Other and to find not a compromise but a *new way* that works for both of them. (More on that later.) Compromise implies that I give up some part of me. That seldom works for very long. Especially when that part of me is one of the parts my partner fell in love with.

I got one more phone message from Victoria. All she said was "This is Victoria. Thank you."

Beginner's Mind

A fundamental practice in Zen Buddhism is that of "beginner's mind," by which is meant the capacity to see the world (and our partner) as if for the first time. We can begin to do so by clearing our minds of the assumption that we "know" who our partner is. This concept is illustrated by an oft-told but nonetheless charming tale of the worldly-wise man who came to the hut of a Zen master, asking to become enlightened. The master smiled and set about making tea while the seeker chatted on about how many spiritual paths he had pursued and how much he already knew. When the tea was ready, the man held out his teacup. The master filled it with rich green tea—and kept pouring, the tea spilling over the lip of the cup onto the tatami mats. The man shouted, "Stop pouring! My cup is already full!"

"Just so," said the master, "and when something is full it is useless to keep adding anything more."

Like this man, most of us think we know a lot about who are partner is. We can say what he or she will do in most situations. Consequently, we tend to take who we believe them to be for granted and not to realize how much of what we "see" is our projection onto them. To truly see them, however, we must first empty our minds of preconceptions and see them anew, as if for the first time, as if we were just beginning to learn about them.

Exercise

Take a few minutes to set this book aside (after you have read this exercise). Close your eyes, take a few deep breaths, and relax as fully as you can. If you wish, go back in your memory to the day on which you first saw your partner. See him or her as you saw them on that day. See hair, eyes, face, hands, body. What first attracted you to them? How do you feel, meeting them for the first time? What qualities of personality do you find attractive?

What was it like, getting to know this person, and falling in love? How did you spend your time together? What did you talk about? How was it to kiss for the first time? To make love for the first time? Take as much time as you want to enjoy these memories.

Now how do you feel inside your body? How do you feel toward your partner?

Isn't that a fun exercise? I recommend that you do it often. It will help you step into the beginner's mind that you had when you first met your partner.

What we are headed for is being able to see our partner anew each day, each minute, as the magical being that he or she really is. Of course he or she is imperfect—that is part of being human. Rather than hoping they will be perfect—or trying to sculpt them into perfection—our job is to see them as they truly are, warts and all, and to develop our own capacity for toleration and acceptance. This process will be easier if we remind ourselves that at the core of anyone there is a Great Mystery, as mysterious as the universe itself.

As you develop your ability to see more and more deeply into an Other, you develop your ability to see more deeply into the Great Mystery of the universe.

Summary

Take a good hard look at who you're with. If your partner is a serial killer or makes their money bilking senior citizens of their Social Security checks, you might consider divorce. If you're worse off with your partner than alone, leave. If you decide to stay, start seeing who they really are, with beginner's mind, as opposed to the ghosts of who your primary caregivers were or who you'd like your partner to become, and develop your capacity to accept. One definition of love is letting the other be who they are.

At the same time, start looking at yourself honestly. Don't put yourself down, either. Observe yourself with compassion. Let yourself be who you are.

> C.O.A.L.: Look at your partner and yourself with Curiosity, Observation, Acceptance, and Love.

6: LISTEN!

Listening is love.
–Jerry Jampolsky

Two extremely helpful life skills are (1) being able to listen to what's going on inside ourselves and (2) accurately decoding what others are truly saying to us. How often—and how well—do you listen to your inner being? Are you at least as aware of what's inside as what's outside?

Exercise

Notice that you are already listening to *yourself* more astutely when you ask yourself how you are feeling or practice chaotic meditation. Deepen this habit by giving yourself alone time without any distraction to tune in to yourself. I suggest that you make it a daily practice to shut the door, turn off the phone, and sit or lie down and breathe deeply. Free your mind from its incessant chatter. Tune into your body. What *sensations* are you aware of within? Scan yourself as a PET scan would, starting at the head and slowly working your way down, a segment at a time. Breathe yet more deeply into any discomforts. Is there anything a bodily part is asking for? For instance, is that sore shoulder aching to be rubbed? What can you do about that?

Next, how are you *feeling* inside? At a basic level, pleasant or unpleasant? If pleasant, breathe into that pleasantness and let it fill your body. If unpleasant, breathe into that and be with it awhile without judging the feeling or yourself. Where do you feel it, *in your body*? When you isolate the feeling, get a sense of it as being mad, sad, or afraid. For instance, I might be feeling uncomfortable. As I stay with this discomfort, I say, aloud, "I'm scared!" Say it a few times. Stay focused on the feeling. Don't think about it—don't judge, analyze, blame. Notice what happens to the feeling.

Now, what do you need around this feeling? First, from yourself. I might *think*, "Gosh, I'm getting low on cash. I can postpone buying that new car/suit/book."

Are there any decisions to be made based upon listening to yourself in this way? For example, I might *decide* to save a lot of money by not getting the car and putting some of it toward a massage for my shoulder.

In sum: Breathe, sense, feel, think, decide.

Now that you've begun listening to your still, small voice within, also begin listening to your partner. I know, you think you already do. Well, read on. *Most of the issues in relationship are magnified by ineffective listening skills.* The basic problem lies in the fact that, while we assume we know how to listen, we don't. No one taught us these fundamental skills.

Back in grad school I heard about a shocking experiment. Researchers focused on couples who said that they had been happily married for at least five years. They took aside one member of the couple and gave him or her a fairly specific message to convey to the partner, for instance, "Let's go out for anchovy pizzas at Joe's Pizzeria tonight around seven." After the couple conferred, they separated them again. The speaker was asked to write down what she thought she had communicated. The listener wrote down what he had heard.

What percentage of the time do you imagine these two written statements coincided, at least roughtly? A simple, unemotional message between two happily married people? 90%? 75%?

Somewhat to their shock, the researchers found that there was good understanding only *20%* of the time. That's one in five cases that the happy couples actually communicated effectively. Imagine what happens when the message is highly emotional.

The sad and somewhat frightening truth is that most of us don't understand each other most of the time.

Rather than assume that we will understand, we need to assume that understanding is a challenge. It requires being present and mindful. And, before we can listen at all, we have several important steps to take. The first is to make a date to communicate.

Before the Communication Session

The person who asks for the communication is the Speaker; the partner is the Listener. It's important to know who is filling which role at any given time.

If you are the Speaker, rather than simply launch into sending a message when your partner is heading out the door, check with your partner to *see if this is a good time for him or her to listen to you.* Give your listener an approximation of how much time you'd like to be listened to. Ten seconds to make sure he knows its reduced-fat milk you want him to pick up? Or twenty minutes to clear a misunderstanding? In effect, you are asking for a date.

As the Listener, check yourself out honestly: Do I really want to be a listener right now? In the middle of the Super Bowl? With the score tied?

It is *really* better to say, "Now's not a great time for me. How about at eight o'clock this evening when the game's over?"

In other words, come back with a counter-proposal for a time when you know you will be able to be a better listener.

Many people rebel at this suggestion. They believe that being in relationship means never having to ask for attention. Yet even in all the marriage vows I've witnessed or spoken, I've never heard anyone promise to be fully attentive 24/7. No human being can do that. If we truly want our partners to hear and understand us, we need to accept that they can do so at some times better than at others, and, that if we *ask* respectfully for some of their time to really listen to us, we're much more likely to be heard.

The meta-message we give when we ask for some listening time from a partner is: I respect your time as a separate person and don't assume that you are simply an extension of myself. Also, I respect myself enough to want to be truly heard when I have something important to say.

I have to admit that sometimes it truly doesn't matter to us whether our partner is paying close attention. As she aged, my mother would tell long and convoluted stories about her friends' lives in Ireland. At first, trying to follow every detail, I was frustrated with her. When I finally realized that it didn't matter to her whether I was following everything, that all she really wanted was a warm body nearby while she could hear her own story, I could be physically present with her and think my own thoughts or meditate. She was perfectly happy with this arrangement. She wanted, as she put it, "to hear myself think." All she needed from me was to stay awake.

If all that you need is a witness while you "hear yourself think," which is a perfectly reasonable request, ask for that. Distinguish that from "I really want you to understand me" or "I'd like to work through our conflict." Be as clear as you can about what you want.

So, as the Speaker I've gotten clear that I really need you to attend to me and I've asked for and gotten a pledge that you will give me twenty minutes of your valuable time to do just that. I'm already feeling good about us because I've been able to ask directly for what I want and you are willing to give to me in this way.

The next step is to prepare for the communications date. Since the Speaker has told you what the topic is, you can clear your body of any old feelings you might be carrying around, using chaotic meditation. *This is the most important preparation you can do.* Once you've cleared your old feelings so you know what you want, it'll be relatively easy to clear your mind.

Clear your mind

As was the case with the know-it-all whose cup was overfull of tea, we cannot really hear someone when our mind is full of something else. How often have you been thinking about what you have to do this morning as you gather your belongings to head out the door when your partner says something about picking up a quart of milk (or something) on your way home? Because you are focused on what's important to you, you fail to register what's important to your partner.

Or, to take another case, what happens when you are whipped with fatigue from a long day and your partner wants you to hear a long story about what happened at work or with the baby? And then gets mad at you for not following the gist of the tale.

And how many times have you been in the middle of an argument when you find yourself focusing on composing your counter-argument while your partner is still talking—and you no longer know what he or she is really saying?

As the Listener, you might think you have to interrupt me to point out that one of my facts is incorrect or to suggest an elegant solution to my problem. You might believe it is up to you to be the Devil's Advocate for my boss and to point out his side of things. Please clear your mind of these incorrect assumptions. They will make you a very poor listener.

These are just a few examples of what gets between our own minds and our partner's words. I'm sure you can add a few others.

The less static you have in your body and brain, the better a Listener you will be. The next skill to master is how to zip your lip and be attentively aware of your partner—not just her words, but everything about her.

Attentive Awareness

I learned Attentive Awareness from Granddad when I was a boy. Although he never said it, I knew absolutely that he loved me deeply. He liked to go for walks or fishing with me. He was always acutely present. He said little, listened much. With him I felt safe to talk about anything. He did not judge me or criticize me. His loving attention was like sunshine to the young flower of my soul. In Granddad's presence I could feel the connection of our essential selves—our Essence. Let me try to make this vague concept clearer.

Attentive Awareness is being fully present with another human being, without having an agenda for them. You aren't trying to teach them anything or change them in any way. You come from your deepest, most compassionate self in empathy with them. You are simply being with them in loving connection, allowing your

Essence, your heart, to join with theirs. You don't have to say a word. In fact, chatter can get in the way.

Most of us, and especially writers like me, attach far too much importance to words. When we think of getting to know someone, we usually imagine doing that through conversation. This is akin to getting to know a wolf by studying its howls and growls.

If you really wanted to get to know a wolf, you would build the animal's trust by being non-aggressive but present. Then you would observe the wolf closely. You would spend every day simply watching what the wolf did, how it interacted with other wolves, how it hunted, how it played with its pups, how it related to you. What you would not do is to expect it to speak to you, nor would you suggest a Freudian diagnosis for it to consider. Unless you are insane, you would not try to turn it into a vegetarian.

You would accept the wolf as it was and be interested in getting to know its behavior.

If you think this idea is far-fetched, rent the wonderful movie *Never Cry Wolf* and treat yourself to a remarkable evening. Or, if you prefer, read the book of the same title. It's a true story.

What can we learn from the author of that book, Farley Mowatt, and other students of animal behavior? First, they do not try to change the animal they're studying. Knowing that their very presence will impact the animal's behavior, they treat it with respect and attempt to minimize their profile. (Unless they are testing how wolves respond to territorial markings, as Mowatt did, in a very funny scene.) Second, they are curious. They truly want to know about this fellow creature. So, three, they observe, carefully.

If you think of your partner not as a tame human but a wild animal, what animal would he or she be? Can you see the wolf or the rabbit or bear in him or her?

Watch what they do, without judgment, in all sorts of different situations. Gather a wealth of observations. Imagine how, if you were in their shoes, you might feel.

Exercise

Ask your partner to talk about anything while you just listen for five or ten minutes. How is it for you to zip your lip and not say a word? Now reverse roles. How is it for you to be attended to without words? Afterwards, take a few minutes to say how it was for you in each role. What do you learn?

We can "listen" to someone's behavior. We can track the content of their words. We can imagine what they are feeling, using the neurons in our brains that mirror theirs. We can also listen to their non-verbal communication.

We are always communicating, even when we don't speak. A wise man once said, "We cannot not communicate."[16] We send a host of signals in our facial expressions, our body language, even the rate of our breathing. Unconsciously or consciously, others pick up these signals—and usually misinterpret them. As you explore your partner, a major learning will be to be able to estimate with increasing accuracy what he or she is feeling based on these nonverbal communications.

Of course you won't rely upon guesswork alone, for projection will skew your perceptions. By continually observing and then *checking out your observation*, you will gradually develop a clearer sense of what your partner is feeling and needing. Later, we'll go more deeply into feelings and how to check out your observations. Right now, let's take a look at needs.

16 Watzlawick, Beavins, and Jackson, *Pragmatics of Human Communication* (1967).

Listening for 'Needs'

I put "needs" in quotes because I'm using the word imprecisely in the lay sense of "something really important to me." The actual denotation of "need" as a noun is those necessities without which I cannot live: Air, water, food, and so forth. An infant needs touch or it will die; an adult can survive without touch, however unhappily. Most adults have a strong desire for loving touch. But since unhappy adults often leave relationships, perhaps I can get away with the stronger word, need, for these are factors without which relationships often perish.

What should not be a surprise to you, if you've read this far, is that different people have different relationship needs. Here again people vary in what suits them. For instance, some people have a strong desire *to hear loving words and frequent validation*, "I love yous" and "Atta-boys." Others are moved less by words than by actions, by *acts of service* such as a lovingly-prepared meal or taking care of the accounting or servicing the car. Still others have a powerful need for *touch*, within or outside of sexuality.

Gary Chapman wrote a helpful book about this called *The Five Languages of Love* (1992). He points out that each of us has a primary and a secondary "love language" that communicates love to us. In addition to the three languages listed above, he includes *sharing quality time* and material *gifts*. His point is that if we truly wish to show our partner love, we need to do it in *their* language rather than ours. If I'm showing you acts of service by stacking the wood for winter and changing the oil in the cars but what you really want is for me to spend quality time with you rather than the wood or the cars, both of us will become frustrated and come to believe the other doesn't really love us.

Just reading these labels, you probably have a good idea what your primary and secondary love languages are. What do you think your partner's are?

If you're unsure what your and your partner's languages of love are, buy Gary's book, fill in his Personal Assessment questionnaire, and, by all means, read the book. Most couples find this is a fun book to discuss. As you become more aware of your partner's core needs, you will be able to listen for them running like an underground river through whatever he or she says. In time, each of you will be able to go directly to labeling whatever basic need it is that you are asking your partner to meet. Being able to do so saves a lot of time.

When you are carefully attending to another person, you are aware not just of the words they happen to be saying, but the deeper connection between you in Essence, their feelings, and their needs. When you do so, the other person will have a sense that you are truly loving them. And, in fact, you are. Listening in this way is a very loving act.

Once you have listened with attentive awareness to your partner's feelings, needs, wishes, body language, and Essence, you can now move to the next step, that of summarizing what you've just heard, the next and crucial part of the listening process, which I call....

The Magic Mirror

There was in ancient Greece a horrible snake-haired creature called the Gorgon. If anyone looked at her, he or she was turned to stone. Our word "petrified" comes from an archaic word meaning, "being turned into stone."

You may have had the experience of feeling so paralyzed around someone that you can't even speak. For you, that person was a Gorgon.

One of Perseus' tasks was to slay the Gorgon, which, believe me, he wasn't looking forward to, so he asked Athena, goddess of wisdom, to help him. She gave him a sharp sword and a burnished shield and some wise guidance.

"Do not look directly at the Gorgon, or you shall turn to stone. Hold up your shield and look into it to see her reflection only. Thus you shall be able to deal with her."

If you want to know what happened you'll have to read the story. For our purposes we can use Athena's wisdom and make it our own. When we stare directly into the eyes of a person we see as Gorgon-like, or even a loving partner we don't know what to say to, we might feel paralyzed. But like Perseus each of us carries a burnished shield given to us by the goddess of wisdom that will act as a mirror and a protection. My job here is to remind you that you always carry it with you.

When we take someone's words personally we freeze up, as if paralyzed by snake venom. What we need, immediately, is a little psychological distance from them. But how can we gain that distance when we are frightened or angry or grief-stricken by what we perceive as a personal attack? Or simply paralyzed with the fear of not being able to do it right for the partner? We use our Magic Mirror, the shield of Athena.

Whatever someone says to you, instead of focusing upon your hurt feelings or what kind of snappy comeback you can retaliate with, simply *reflect* their words to them. For example:

"You're a jerk!"
"You think I'm a jerk?"

This deceptively simple technique does about 300 things simultaneously. Let's look at a very few of them for right now.

First, it breaks our paralysis and gives us a response that doesn't take a lot of thought. We aren't standing there like a stone statue. We can say something that's not a counterattack. We are practicing verbal non-violence.

Second, it buys us a little more time to deal with our feelings about the statement.

Third, and most importantly, *it shows the speaker that we have heard him or her*. This part is crucial. As we learned earlier, without this kind of reflection, 80% of what's being said will be miscommunicated. By taking the time to reflect what we heard, we do our part to catch such ineffective communications. Often, when I reflect in this way, the speaker, hearing what she just said, will change the communication. For example, when I reflect that she called me a jerk she might amend:

"Well, what I mean is I'm mad at you right now."

She's now moved from a verbal attack to revealing important information about her internal state. It's much easier for me to hear that than the attack, so by using my Magic Mirror I've managed to help us move to a softer tone. Further, if she *does* mean to attack me, she knows I've gotten that message and won't have to keep saying the same thing over and again.

> When people *know* they are being heard, *and the only way they can truly know it is when we reflect their words to them,* they tend to be soothed by the fact that they have been attended to without an attack.

I use a verbal attack situation first because it fits more clearly with the Gorgon story. I'm sure we've all experienced how our sweet loving partners turn into Gorgons once in awhile. But what about when it's a case of the sweetie asking for us to pick up a quart of milk? Do we need to use the Magic Mirror then?

You bet. Look at this example:

"Could you pick up a quart of milk for me?"
"You'd like a quart of milk."
"Did I say quart? I meant a half gallon. Reduced fat."
"A half gallon of reduced fat milk. I'm on it."
"Oh, I feel so loved when you pay such close attention to me!"

Another benefit of the Magic Mirror is precisely that: We feel soothed and loved by being attended to so carefully.

Notice a couple other benefits. If I'd brought home a quart of milk, probably whole milk, I'd be faced with a frustrated wife who was *certain* she'd made it clear that she wanted a half gallon. Equally certain that I'd heard her say "quart" I'd be likely to get frustrated myself:

"Geez-Louise! I try to do you a favor by leaving work early to get the milk you wanted and instead of thanks I get a load of grief about how I never listen to you and..."

How many arguments like this one, where each partner is sure of what was said but doesn't agree on what was actually said, have you been in? What's that done for your blood pressure? For your relationship? *Every one of those frustrating arguments could have been avoided by the use of your Magic Mirror*

He Said, She Said

As an aside, I'd like to say here that I counsel my couples to stay away from these futile arguments over who said or did what when. Unless you have high-quality audio-video footage of the scene you will never reach a satisfying conclusion to such arguments. What is at stake is not just who has a more accurate memory but our very ability to process reality and remember it, which most people have a deep investment in believing must be accurate. It's frightening to have to admit that our reality-processing apparatus is flawed. As Nietzsche put it succinctly:

> When Pride and Memory have a debate, Pride always wins.

Instead, agree to disagree about the past and shift your focus to the future. Rather than argue futilely over whether you said "quart" or "half-gallon," *what do we need to do in the future to prevent such misunderstandings*? That simple but effective substitution will move you from being angry and bitter adversaries to being teammates approaching a common problem. Your good brainpower is better employed in finding an elegant solution together than in trying to make your partner wrong.

> Would I rather be right or would I rather be happy?

Returning to our discussion of the Magic Mirror—don't take my word for it. Take it for a test drive for three weeks. Reflect your partner's (and your children's, if you have children) words, wishes, and feelings back to them. Check out how often you prevent misunderstanding. Watch how people respond to knowing, absolutely, that they are heard.

At first you'll feel like a foolish parrot. That's okay. Any new behavior takes a while to integrate. (Remember when you were first learning to ride a bicycle?) It's fine to summarize back in your own words, too, although you'll find, I think, that some words are magical for the person who spoke them. Especially feeling words. For instance:

"I'm really frustrated right now!"
"You're feeling angry now."
"NO! I'm frustrated!!"
"You're not angry, you're frustrated."
"You got it."

When you can use your Magic Mirror to reflect back Magic Words, you've got a sure winner.

Myriad Benefits of the Magic Mirror

You'll find many uses and benefits to this disarmingly simple technique, if you use it sincerely. A sarcastic tone will sabotage a great many things, including this. So only use your Mirror when you truly want to reach an understanding with someone. If you really don't care about them, they'll intuit that and react to the non-caring.

This technique, which many of you will already have some familiarity with, is now widely used—in business, in the police, in the military, between parent and child, teacher and student. It was popularized by the great American psychologist Carl Rogers.[17]

The military always uses the Mirror. When the newly minted Second Lieutenant says, "Sarge, I want you to take the hill at 0600."

17 *On Becoming a Person* (1995).

Sarge says, "Yessir, take the hill at 0600 sir."

And the looie says, "Oops. No, 0600 is the air strike and artillery barrage. I think we better go in at 0630."

"Good thinking, sir. Hate to have all that iron on our heads on the way up."

Lives that might have been tragically lost are saved.

The first usage of the Magic Mirror was to prevent unnecessary deaths, back in the days of sailing ships. Used well today it can prevent the death of relationship.

Check It Out (CIO)

My rule of thumb is: *When in doubt, check it out.*

In itself the Magic Mirror serves as a checkpoint, for rather than assuming I hear you I am offering my reflection of what I heard so you can correct me if I got it wrong (or was starting the attack on the hill too soon).

Once I know you know I've heard you, I have an opportunity to check out anything I might be puzzled about. For instance, the sergeant from the prior example might want to check out that we're talking about Heartbreak Hill or some other hill. Does "take it" mean to drive the enemy off the top? Or all the way back to the Yalu? Once we take it are we supposed to occupy it—or head back to base for a hot shower?

Similarly, in the example of picking up the milk, it's wise to check out how much of what specific kind the Speaker is requesting.

When John Alden went to woo Priscilla Mullins on behalf of his friend, Captain Miles Standish, back in the Plymouth Colony in 1621, Priscilla said, famously, "Speak for yourself, John." A lesser man might have let the comment pass. John checked it out, married Priscilla, and lived happily ever after. What might have happened if Capt. Standish had checked it out for himself rather than sending an emissary?

In what other ways can you check something out with your partner? After you have been attentively aware, observed widely and imagined deeply, and mirrored what you have understood about them in their own words, then—and only then—you can move to check out with them *what you are curious about.*

For instance, you might say, "I really want to know you deeply, and I'm curious about something I've observed. When your mother comes to visit, I notice that you say much less than you usually do—and nothing about politics or religion. I imagine that you're being careful not to offend her. Is that the case?"

Or: "I'd like to understand you better. I notice that when I come up and give you a big kiss, you want to go to the bedroom with me. I imagine that you think my kissing you means I want to have sex. Is that right?"

The important attitude here is one of loving curiosity. If you think he's being a wimp with his mother or she's excessively randy, that kind of judgment will skew the resulting discussion. Especially if your intent in bringing up the observation is to remake your partner in some way—if you really wish he'd tell his mother she's a religious bigot or that you really think she's oversexed. We'll get to how to ask for a change in behavior, which is something completely different. What we're talking about here is listening, in the broadest sense of that word, with an open heart.

An Attitudinal Shift

The astute reader will have noticed that undergirding these simple techniques for effective listening is a shift in the user's attitude from "I know exactly how things are!" to "I'm becoming humbler about how things actually are." From being an arrogant know-it-all in possession of the Truth to someone who accepts that every human being has tremendous limitations upon their ability to see and hear and intuit. We move from a firm belief that "The way I see and hear it is the way it is!" to "This is the way I see it, but I could be looking through tinted spectacles, and I'm interested in how you might see it." The reality of a baseball umpire has no place in a relationship. At the root level there is a huge change of consciousness possible here which enables someone to let go of insisting on his or her reality and be open to new possibilities. When we can make this attitudinal shift and listen without judgment we will discover that your partner is a rich and undiscovered country.

For most people, that is not an easy shift. Most of us are quite attached to the belief that our sensory perceptions are providing us with accurate input. It's frightening to consider the possibility that our senses might be somewhat flawed or that we might be projecting. After all, if I can't trust what I see and hear, what can I trust?

Human beings have a strong psychological need to be anchored in a reality that makes sense to them. When we come to the brink of a differing reality, we'll tend to become fearful and to resist it. Most people resisted the idea for a very long time that the world could be round. They were fearful that if they explored the margins of the known maps they might fall off the edges of a flat Earth.

Even a glancing look at history demonstrates that many people are quite willing to kill others, or fight to the death, rather than even consider that one of their beliefs might be incorrect. Think, for instance, of all the human beings tortured and killed because of religious beliefs. Jonathan Swift satirized this human tendency in *Gulliver's Travels* in a trenchant passage describing the awful wars fought between the Big Enders and the Little Enders, referring to which end of the soft boiled egg each thought it appropriate to spoon the egg from. Yet how far is this fictional silliness from the fact that human beings are ready to kill or die over whether or not one should eat the meat of the pig or the cow?

Similar violent disagreement over fairly petty matters occurs in most coupleships. I have listened to far too many couples debate passionately over the sacred position of the toilet seat or whether the towels should be folded in halves or in thirds. I find it fascinating how few people realize that the way they believe things should be is mostly a function of how their family of origin did things when they were growing up.

I followed the toilet seat debate in Ann Landers' column for much of one year. The furor of the arguments astounded me. I enjoyed the egalitarian view of one person who kept the following plaque in his pizza parlor's unisex bathroom: "Will the gentlemen please lower the seat for the ladies; will the ladies please raise the seat for the gents." There was a lot less balance from most writers, who seemed to feel as passionately about the position of the seat as some people feel about the correct name for God.

Then a widow wrote in. While I don't have her exact words in front of me, she said, if I remember aright, something like this:

> *For our forty years of marriage I nagged my husband to leave the toilet seat down. He often forgot. There it stood, over and again, like a flag of defiance every time I walked past the bathroom. We got into some bitter arguments about it. He died from a heart attack three years ago. Now the seat is always down. I would give anything, now, to walk past the bathroom and see the seat up again.*

The opportunity that lies before you is to accept and cherish each other for the time you have together. That time might end today. If you knew that it would, how would you want to listen to your partner? How would you want him or her to listen to you?

OK, enough theory. Now, put what you're learning into practice with the next exercise.

Exercise

Sit comfortably and look directly at me. Eyeball to eyeball. Shuttle your point of consciousness from what I am saying back inside yourself to your own breathing and then back to me again. Zip your lip. Say nothing. Listen as totally as you can. When thoughts arise—which will happen—gently bid them to leave and bring yourself back to your breath and then my words. Use your body to sense how I am feeling and you mind to deduce what you think is the essence of what I am trying to communicate. You need not get every word—you are not a tape recorder. Instead, what is the big picture?

When you don't follow something, just let it go. Give me the chance to speak my piece. As I am able to do so, without interruption, I will "hear myself think" and come to some new understandings that I didn't have before we sat down. This is an extremely valuable part of being attended to with awareness. And, as you listen to the big picture, pieces will tend to fall into place.

When it looks like I've finished, give me another minute—another thought may occur to me. When I finally smile and say, "That's about it. Thanks for listening." you can take that as my belief that I'm done.

Now use your Magic Mirror to reflect to me what you've understood me to be trying to communicate. What is the essence of what I'm saying? What are my core needs? Do the best you can without expecting yourself to be perfect. This is not a test. It's an ongoing recalibration. Hearing you mirroring my words may well help me refine my thoughts. Be open to my making changes or adding amendments. Just keep reflecting until you notice that I seem to relax and say something like, "You've got it. Thanks."

What triggers your love?

Here is an exercise that you will have fun doing and that will add a lot to your relationship:

"I feel loving when..."

What actions by your partner spark that loving feeling in you? Write down as many *specific behaviors* that she or he does—from greeting you with a warm smile to making love with you—that signal "love" to you that you can think of in the next 5-10 minutes. The more specific and petty the better. I was amazed to discover that I felt an almost overwhelming feeling of love suffuse my body when, during our dating days, Yashi made me some sandwiches wrapped in waxed paper for my trip home from a visit to her. I remembered that my mother had done the same with my school lunches when I was a boy.

Okay, now go back and rate each of these behaviors from 1-10, with 1 meaning "I feel a love twinge" to 10 meaning "Waddanda!"

What do you notice as you examine your list? What do you find out about yourself that you might not have known before?

You might want to suggest that your partner do the same exercise. Then trade lists. (You can always ask for it back to add to or change items on your list.) I keep Yashi's in my desk drawer. When I feel loving toward her and want to show her that, I think, "By gum, I'll take her to a Giant's game!" However, when I examine her list, I fail to find "I feel loving when...he takes me to a baseball game" anywhere on it. Aha, I think. I must be projecting: I would feel loving if she took *me* to a Giant's game. But I do want to show her some love—what can I do? I know women like flowers.

I'll bring her some flowers. I check out her list again. There it is! "I feel loving when...he brings me flowers." But when I glance at the point total for this expensive present, I find a skinny "1." Right below it, however, I find, "I feel loving when...he comes to me and gives me a big hug." And it scores 8 points! I run into the kitchen, tell her I love her (6 points) and give her a giant hug, knowing I have just deposited a lot of gold into the Love Bank.

By doing this exercise, which I have adapted from one of Harville Hendrix's, you are first listening to yourself (in doing it) and then listening to your partner (in reading his or her list). Writing to one another and reading what your partner says is another way of listening. It is often helpful, when you find yourselves stuck in some attempt to understand and be understood, to shift out of the customary verbal communication to a written one.

Some Other Ways to Listen to Yourself

I want to encourage you to find several different ways to listen to yourself as well as to your partner, mirroring what you hear. When you lie down for some "chaotic meditation" make sure you are expressing yourself vocally so you can hear yourself. When you hear your words and sounds, you will gain insight into what is going on with you.

Second, use pencil and paper to write out your innermost thoughts and feelings in a journal. No, do not use your word processor. Why? Because the physical movements of the writing hand and arm triggers deeper areas of the brain and helps you access them. I am continually astounded by what comes out of the end of my pencil. I didn't realize I thought or felt it until I see it in black and white.

Third, make it a practice to take a few minutes at least a couple of times a day to check in with yourself. Scan your body and check for any areas of delight or discomfort. Ask yourself what you're feeling right now. If the answer is "Fine" dig a little deeper.

Check out the basic feeling groups of sad, mad, glad, and afraid. Such signposts, however clumsy they are, can help us know ourselves.

Come up with your own ways of attending to yourself and to your partner. You will be amazed by the richness of the inner world within each of you.

Checklist for Effective Listening

1. The Speaker asks to be heard. Make a mutually convenient date. Ask for a specific amount of time at a specific time for a *single, specific topic.*
2. Prepare for the communications date. Clear your body of old feelings and your mind of chatter.
3. Be attentively aware. Zip your lip. Do not dispute. Listen and absorb. What do you imagine are the core needs beneath what she is saying?
4. When the Speaker feels finished, give her a minute. Ask if she is done for now. Then use your Magic Mirror to reflect to her the essence of what you've heard.
5. Be open to the Speaker's needing to refine what she is attempting to communicate. Keep reflecting her amendments until you hear, "Yes. You've got it. Thank you."
6. *After* you've gotten this signal that she feels good about having been listened to, check out anything you have questions about. Request any additional information that will help you understand her better. Reflect her additions.
7. Once you think you are both as clear as you can be today, thank your partner for sharing this information with you.

8. If you wish to respond, make a separate date for that. I suggest taking at least a small break between listening sessions.
9. If the going gets too rough, either partner can say, "I need a break. Can we come back to this at ____" Agree to a second round sometime within 24 hours.

PART III: FEELINGS

Our feelings are what give value and meaning to our lives and especially to our relationships. Yet few of us in America today live a healthy feeling life. Many of us learned to clamp down the flow of feeling and are fearful of it. Others choose to dramatize the slightest feeling into an opera. Unfortunately, only a few of us grew up in an environment capable of allowing us healthy expression of feeling. In our culture, far from getting a solid education in feelings, we are taught to suppress, twist, and pervert them. In order to have successful relationships, most of us will need to undergo a remedial education program in feeling.

We need to learn to pay compassionate attention to them within our bodies.

We need to learn how to excavate and remove old, held feelings from the deep freeze of unconsciousness.

And we need to learn how to process them in the now as a couple.

7: ATTEND TO YOUR FEELINGS

I wouldn't know a feeling
if it bit me in the butt.
–a client

We need to be gently compassionate with ourselves around our feelings. We have grown up in a feeling-phobic and largely unconscious culture called modern America, a generally painful experience (when we are aware of it), that has given us the message that our feeling selves are not very welcome and that we shouldn't pay much attention to feelings anyway.

Do you remember some of the messages, verbal and nonverbal, that you got around feelings as you were growing up? Here's a handful that I hear, over and again, as I work with my clients:

"Don't be a crybaby. Big boys/girls don't cry."
"Don't be afraid. There's nothing to be afraid of."

"You must learn to control yourself or you'll end up in prison."
"Smile and the world smiles with you, frown and you frown alone."

Add a couple of your own.

Imagine how it would have been for you if your caregivers had instead reacted to your expressions of feelings more positively:

"It's okay to cry when you're sad. Crying gets the sadness out."
"It's scary for you when Daddy's late picking you up."
"You got really mad at that boy!"
"I can see you're upset right now."

The meta-message here is that feelings are quite normal, a part of being human. You would also be learning to match a label to the feeling you are having.

Sadly, from early childhood on, most of us were conditioned to repress our feelings. Some of us do that very effectively now, avoiding feelings in ourselves and others. Others of us rebel and dramatize feelings. We are consequently a society of Avoiders and Dramatizers, often in the same relationship.

Rather than engage in that fruitless struggle, we can accept that we are pretty much all wounded products of a culture that has big trouble with feelings and begin to do something positive about it. A first step is to be compassionately attentive toward ourselves and our partners. Begin by simply focusing your attention inward and observing what you are aware of without judgment or any attempt to change what you find. As with any activity you wish to improve in, you will need to budget time.

Create Alone Time

Our feeling selves are amazingly resilient. Just by giving yourself time alone during which you become mindful of what is occurring within, you will recover huge tracts of feeling. The challenge is to prevent yourself from distracting. Most of us are superb distracters.

Primal therapy, which is the most effective tool for recovering our feeling selves that I know of, begins with a three-week period (the Intensive) in which one does nothing but focus on feelings. A primary tool for helping feelings arise is to take away our customary distractions. To this end, clients stay not at home surrounded by family and supportive objects but alone in a boring hotel room. They also receive the following guidelines:

GUIDELINES FOR INTENSIVES

To maximize the effectiveness of your therapy, please cooperate with the following instructions:

1. You already know what you do to avoid your feelings. Don't do it! This includes overeating, keeping busy and on the run, nail-biting, etc.

2. Stop all drugs 48 hours before therapy begins. This includes caffeine, nicotine, alcohol, pot, aspirin, tranquillizers, etc. Continue to abstain throughout the Intensive.

3. 24 hours before your first session, you are to be totally alone without distractions. If you have access to a phone or TV, unplug them. Continue isolation throughout the Intensive unless your therapist indicates otherwise. Talk to no one but your therapist.

4. If you go out to eat, use a minimum of talk to order the meal. (Some clients wear a sticker with "Speech Fast" written on it, so they don't have to explain to someone why they're not speaking and write out their food wishes.) Eat

lightly of nutritious foods. Listen to what your body wants to eat or drink. Do not eat two hours prior to a session.

5. Do not meditate, masturbate, oversleep, or exercise.

6. Do no reading or writing unless you are instructed to do so.

7. Let your feelings ascend. Go into them whenever they come up, except within two hours of your session.

8. Confer with your therapist if you are having problems following these Guidelines.

• • •

Take a moment, right now, to set this book aside for a few minutes and ask yourself how simply reading over those guidelines leaves you feeling.

• • •

What I found during my own Intensive was that just by stepping out of my workaday life and providing myself with three weeks of time and space to focus within that my feelings began coming up into consciousness almost immediately. I would find my mind attempting to distract me from my feelings, over and over, through a variety of cunning maneuvers. One particularly seductive one was that I kept thinking of the most amazingly creative ideas for novels, plays, poems—I might forget them! Surely it wouldn't hurt to make a brief note?

An enormous amount of our time and energy (and money) is spent on distracting ourselves from our real feelings. Think of all the addictions, from alcohol and drugs to gambling and workaholism. Think of the compulsions to do, to shop, to buy, to be online, and, yes, to write.

When we choose to step off the merry-go-round, for three weeks or for ten minutes, and simply let ourselves *be*, with no place to go, nothing to do, no problem to solve, we can stop the "monkey mind" from chattering and allow the deeper, realer part of us to emerge.

Those three weeks that I gave myself to engage in this process were the most precious of my life. I sat in a stark hotel room with a view of an airshaft, eating peanut butter sandwiches. It was a real treat to walk the three blocks from the hotel to the Center everyday for my therapy session—the only time I got to talk! Until my therapist told me to stop the words and just make sounds. During those weeks I had a love affair—with myself. To my surprise I discovered that I had an incredibly rich inner life that was endlessly fascinating.

Doris Lessing wrote a novel in which a woman locks herself in her apartment for three weeks and sobs, screams, and pounds out her long-stuffed feelings. I know of several people who have managed a similar process. While it is certainly better than not touching one's feelings at all, the guidance of a good therapist is invaluable.

Not everyone is cut out for a three week Intensive. Begin with twenty minutes a day. Call it mediation if you wish. Go into a quiet, darkened place and sit quietly, observing your mind and your breathing. Welcome the feelings that come up for you.

Develop Your Awareness

Most of us were taught to pay more attention to what is outside of us than to what is inside. We need to begin to correct that imbalance. Start right now. Bring your attention to what's happening inside your body. Shut your eyes if that helps you focus within. Scan through your body for any physical sensations, aches or pains, places of tension or tight muscles, feelings of warmth or coolness, well-being or unease. Are your teeth clenched, jaw tight? Is there a knot in the pit of your stomach? How deep, or shallow, is your breathing?

In the same way that you can be aware of the clock ticking in the room or the hawk circling overhead, you can use your inner eye to become more aware of what's inside. Here's an exercise to help you do just that. Start with both inside and outside awareness. This is a good exercise to do with a partner, if possible.

Exercise

"Now I am aware...."

Sit facing one another. Take a minute to tune in to yourself. Then say what you are aware of as it floats into your awareness. As the Listener, my job is to simply connect with you through Attentive Awareness, without saying anything. After five minutes, switch roles.

How was that for you, to have someone attend to you without saying anything? Where you more attuned to what was outside or inside? What do you think will help you gain greater access to what's inside? How was it to just attend? Was it hard to zip your lip? Talk with your partner about how it was for you in each role. What do you learn about yourself and your partner by doing this exercise together?

Going more deeply within

Here's another exercise to assist you in gaining inner access. Don't read it yet. The best way to do it is to ask your partner or a friend to read it to you while you're lying down, not knowing what's coming. Ask your partner if he or she would give you about twenty minutes to do so. (When the reader sees the instruction to pause, make it a long one, perhaps a minute.)

Prepare the space by turning off all electrical devices and making sure you won't be disturbed. Darken the room by pulling shades and dimming lights. Let yourself lie down flat on your back in some relatively comfortable place like a bed or a blanket on the floor. Begin with a few minutes of deep breathing, paying attention to the three parts of the breath: The inbreath, the outbreath, and the little pause in between, when the mystics tell us our soul is closest to our body.

Exercise

Let yourself close your eyes and breathe deeply. (Pause.) Imagine that you are walking along a country road. Feel the texture of the road underfoot, smell the scents in the air, listen to the sounds around you, see the countryside. (Pause.) As you round a bend in the road, you see, up ahead of you, a large tree. What does it look like? (Pause.)

Beneath the tree, almost in an attitude of waiting, you see a small child. As you come nearer, you see that this child is your younger self. How do you feel when you see your child self? (Pause.)

As you stand before your younger self, what is the one statement that you wish to make that might help him or her in the future which you know better than anyone lies ahead? (Pause.)

Now let yourself be the child looking up at the adult. How do you feel about the person you've grown up into? (Pause.) Is there anything you wish to say to this adult you will become? To ask? (Pause.)

Switch back into the adult you. Kneel down and take your child self into your arms. (Pause.) Feel the smooth skin of the cheek, the soft hair against your face. Pour into this child all the love you know he or she will need for what lies ahead. Breathe together for a time. (Pause.)

When you feel ready, stand up to say goodbye for now, knowing you can always return to this place, this tree, and find your child self waiting for you. How do you feel about parting? (Pause.)

Walk back along the country road, feeling what's happening within. When you reach the place where you began, come back to the feeling of the bed or floor beneath you, take a deep breath, and open your eyes.

You might wish to take a few minutes to jot down some notes to yourself about how this experience was for you. I suggest that you build upon this beginning to deepen the connection with your inner child. Here are some means to do so:

1) Find a photograph of yourself from about that age and place it where you will see it every day. Greet the image of your younger self and ask how he or she is. Listen to the answer.

2) Further that dialog by switching into the child consciousness and responding. It helps to do this process out loud. It also helps to move back and forth between two chairs, one for the adult, the other for the child. You might want some privacy to do it.

3) Dialog with your inner child in your journal, in the following manner: Using your dominant hand (the one you usually write with), ask how your little self is and what he or she might need. Switch the pen or pencil into the other hand, and write the reply. Continue, switching hands.

4) Check in with your child during the ups and downs of the day. Ask, "How ya doin'?"

These simple processes will help you gain greater contact with your feeling self. The child has access to much more feeling than the adult. By developing this relationship you will vastly increase your capacity to access how you are feeling. Once you are paying more careful attention to what's happening inside, you will become aware that you have a rich feeling life.

A cheat sheet on feelings

The next step is to select a label that will act as a signpost pointing toward how you are feeling within. Such a label will be helpful to both you and your partner. This is a step that terrifies many a strong-hearted person, many of whom tell me that they wouldn't know a feeling from a fandango. While it's embarrassing to acknowledge how little emotional intelligence one actually has, the truth is that's the case for most of us.

In the interests of remedial emotional education, I have devised a short primer on feelings. Please understand that all such labels are only provisional—you need not be wedded to them. You can always re-label or refine your initial offering. I hope the following section will be helpful.

There are basically *four major feeling groups* that cover about 90% of our most common feelings:

sad, mad, glad, and afrad.

Er, afraid. I was trying to make them all rhyme so they'd be easy to remember.

Let's look at each feeling in turn, with some physical clues to help discriminate them. More than one clue may be present:

Sad: Bodily heaviness, especially in chest and stomach and perhaps in the limbs as well, head tends to droop down, weeping, sobbing, moaning, tightness in throat, tightness in middle-low back.

Mad: Body energized, breathing faster, clenched jaw, hands into fists, arms want to move, legs to kick, sense of heat, voice raised or growling, seeing red, tightness in scapulae.

Glad: Bodily lightness and ease, easy breathing, smiling and laughing, larger movements, lack of tightness, more contactful.

Afraid: Body tense and cool, even rigid or frozen, though legs might want to flee, shoulders hunched, trapezii tight, inhibited breathing, arms protect, eyes either very wide or shut tight, whimpering or screaming.

Is that sufficient to get you started? Add your own descriptions as you become more mindful of how you experience each of these feelings.

When you are observing your own feelings, take a guess at which one of these general groups your feeling might be in. As you become more accustomed to labeling your own feelings, you'll gain more confidence in being able to *provisionally* label others'.

When you are listening for your partner's feelings, take a guess at one of those four and then *check it out* by asking your partner. "I'm wondering if you're sad right now?"

If your partner disagrees, *take him or her at face value.* I would remind you of the very important axiom for good relating: *Each partner gets to be the expert on him or herself.* Even if you don't believe your partner's description of what's happening within, accept it provisionally, giving them the respect of the benefit of the doubt. So when she says,

"No, I'm not sad."

You mirror:

"Oh, you're not sad."

And then zip your lip. They will probably be reconsidering what's going on inside. Do not, ever, suggest that they are lying to you or themselves. That is not a path that will produce connection in 99 cases out of 100. When you consistently accept their self-description, they will, over time, come to feel safe enough to be able to plumb their own feeling and label it for you. For most people, doing so with accuracy takes time and practice, like learning any new skill such as how to bake a cake or drive a Ferrari.

Notice that observing feelings and identifying feelings is a mutually reinforcing process: When I know you're listening I pay more attention to what I might be feeling. As I pay more attention to my feelings, I become more comfortable with them and have a clearer idea of how to label them. We find we discover deeper parts of ourselves that can connect us on a new level that fosters more intimacy. When we both are more accepting toward our feeling selves, our feelings thaw out and no longer have to be shut away in an internal deep freeze. This upward spiral is one that will benefit the relationship as well as the individuals in it.

Why Not Just Keep Feelings Frozen? (What We Don't Know Can't Hurt Us, Right?)

Avoidance is natural in most human beings. We put off the pain of filling out our tax forms or getting a flu shot. Because navigating through feelings is sometimes painful, we will come up with the most ingenious rationalizations one can imagine to justify staying away from our feeling reality. There are even some therapists who do so, quite articulately. They will argue, for instance, that research shows that the more we express anger the angrier we become—so let's avoid anger completely.[18]

That's actually true—*in the short run*. Think about it: You've been told most of your life that you're a bad person if you get angry—that you might injure or kill someone!—and you've been

18 Carol Tavris, *Anger* (1989).

frantically stuffing your anger for years. When it does bust through it's scary—and so you redouble your efforts at stuffing it. Pretty soon you've got a nuclear stockpile big enough to make any bellicose country envious. In therapy, you're given permission to express some of that anger, and—*whoosh!*—out comes a chunk of the backlog. The rest, of course, also wants to thaw and flow downhill, so it rushes toward the new exit—and you find yourself *consciously* angrier than you were when you were stuffing it. Duh. I would point out that *the anger was always there, but in a twisted form*. Now you're getting to it straight.

When a good therapist works with you and tells you it'll get worse before it gets better and helps you set in place structures that protect your loved ones, you get through this stage. When you've dumped enough of the old anger, lo and behold, you find yourself carrying less anger than you ever had in your life. You will also become less passive-aggressive or forgetful.

This may take some time. For me, it took nearly a year of hard work, of individual sessions, group sessions, and a lot of processing on my own. Being a "nice guy," I had a ton of stuffed anger. During that time, I couldn't communicate with my father. (I'd written him to explain that I needed the break to feel my old feelings.) But I got through those old feelings and you will too, if you're willing to work hard at it. I guarantee it. At the end of that time not only had I flushed out most of my old feeling—I could love my father for the first time. For the final two decades of his life we shared a truly good relationship.

What the misguided researchers didn't do is follow the expressers long enough. With any competent feeling therapist, clients are able to learn how to dump their anger safely, without hurting anyone or anything, and to gradually decommission the nuclear stockpile. You don't need to continue to stuff angry feelings or carry that baggage around with you anymore. I have helped hundreds of people free themselves of old anger. Not one of them has killed anyone or beaten anyone up and only two even punched holes in the sheetrock. Not one of them has declared war on an innocent country or strapped on a suicide bomb.

The sense of freedom that comes when you know you can feel angry and express it in a healthy manner without hurting anyone is immensely liberating. One can then consult one's anger as a wise guide rather than see it as a boogeyman.

I am very sad that there are so many people who are so terrified of anger that they feel they have to label it a sin (as does the Catholic Church) or tell us that we must learn to stuff it more effectively (as do certain frightened therapists). Here's an important psychological truth that I have seen corroborated over and again throughout my almost four decades as a therapist:

> When we split off a portion of our feeling selves and label that portion "bad," we simply push it into an underground dungeon where it will grow bestial. There is nothing "bad" about our feelings; they just *are*. They are also transitory. This, too, will pass, unless you lock it in the dungeon. What we might do is to remember that feelings and behavior are not the same thing. Anger is not the same thing as violence. When we can feel our feelings, we don't have to act them out. When we lock them up, they *will* emerge, in sometimes frightening and destructive behavior. They will bite us in the butt.

There is a cogent little tome titled *The Angry Book* (1969) written by Dr. Theodore Isaac Rubin. Dr. Rubin is a psychiatrist who also wrote "Lisa and David," a story about young people in a mental institution who fall in love, which was made into a critically-acclaimed movie called *David and Lisa* (isn't Hollywood brilliant with name changes?). Dr. Rubin, who has worked with many psychotic people and is past president of the American Institute of Psychoanalysis, points out with lucidity what happens to us when we stuff our anger. I often wonder if the therapists who advocate stuffing (which they call "anger management") remember what happens when anger is re-directed and the enormous price we pay for doing so. I won't go into the details here. Read Dr. Rubin's classic.

• • •

If you, gentle reader, detect some annoyance on my part at the "stuff-it" school of therapy, you are quite intuitive. More than once in the history of psychotherapy, a few therapists from Freud on down have aligned themselves with the stuff-it side, thereby demonstrating their own fear of feeling.[19] Since the larger society has been the primary suppressor of feelings, unleashing what Wilhelm Reich called the "emotional plague," it is a sad day when psychotherapists ally themselves with the forces of repression. In the old U.S.S.R., if you set out to change the system you were quite logically ruled insane and put into a mental institution. I become just a tad annoyed when my fellow psychotherapists ally with the suppressors rather than working for the greater liberation of humankind.

However, I do not mean to say that, *once you have felt through most of your old feelings*, there is no place for management techniques, including the old standby of counting to ten. For example, walking away from a situation that you know is highly flammable is clearly excellent advice. The problem I have is the attempt to skip the feeling-through step and going directly to management. That will only work if the feelings are feeble enough to be managed. For those who have a large stockpile and/or are of choleric disposition,

---

19 See Jeffrey Moussaieffe Masson's remarkable true tale about why Freud transmogrified from a feeling-based therapist into a scared, heady one to cover his own tragic mistake in having his patient Emma undergo a botched operation on her nose to cure her sexual problems: *The Assault on Truth: Freud's Suppression of the Seduction Theory* (2003).

the ineffectiveness of the management program leaves them feeling even worse about themselves—and therefore angrier—than they were before. For most of us in the general population, there is no quick fix, no saccharine substitute for doing the herculean labor of working through our old feelings.

It is perhaps the most valuable labor you can do in this lifetime.

8: FEELING THROUGH ON YOUR OWN

One does not become enlightened by imaging figures of light
but by making the darkness conscious.
–Carl Jung

First, a bit of review. How are you doing at being mindful of your feelings on a daily basis? Does it help you to be able to name what you are experiencing? Or are you happy just to feel it? Feelings are mediated mostly through the right half of the brain, while analyzing what you're feeling and assigning it a label is a left-brain function. As you are feeling through you'll probably find you can go deeper into your feelings by staying right-brained, but be mindful of what works best for you.

The next step is to be able to recognize when you are about to be hijacked by archaic feelings and to do something different. What do you usually do when old feelings hijack you? Melinda becomes animated and her voice rises in tone and volume. She wants to "express her feelings" to Sanjit. He will become very quiet and outwardly calm, while dealing with a lot of anxiety inside. He wishes he could hide. Many men have this reaction. Unaware of his anxiety, Melinda hates his appearing so "superior" and is soon screaming at him.

Tom goes out into his shop to try to cool off. After he leaves, his partner, Sandy, goes ice cold and won't talk to him at all for two or three days. After enough time has passed, they gradually resume their normal activities without ever having addressed the issue.

In addition to the fact that you might be acting bizarrely, you can tell an old feeling by its size. Present feelings are moderate and fairly easy to manage. Old feelings are big. When you find yourself in a big feeling, it's probably archaic. Old feelings are also more likely to somatize—to show up in your body. A sudden headache, unexplained physical pains, a stiff neck, your back going out, the sensation of being in an altered state, as if you are living a few inches from your body.

When one partner realizes that a big feeling has just erupted into the middle of the relationship, the best action you can take is to not-do. Resist the powerful urge to fall into your customary patterns, which will be some variation of the fight-flight-freeze response of the reptilian brain. At this point the neocortex is about to be overwhelmed by the more primitive brain stem. As you probably already know, that means that rational dialog is highly unlikely. The best thing you can do is to signal that you need a time out.

Take a Break

You can do so by saying, "I need a time out/break. *I'll be back in 60 minutes* (or some other specific time within 24 hours)." However, that's a lot of words to put together when you're basically a large, agitated lizard. Some couples agree on a code word such as "Mayday" or "Banana cream pie." One couple keeps a red baseball cap on the hall hook and when one of them puts it on they know it means "No talking right now."

By whatever means you do it, the important thing is to have an ironclad agreement that when one of you says "Mayday" you will *absolutely* stop interacting immediately. While people like Tom have no problem doing so, those more like Melinda might find it very hard to cease and desist. If you are one of those who attempt to prolong the interaction after such a signal, you will probably need help from a good therapist to be able to accomplish it. Being able to do so is fundamental to any relationship. Knowing that your partner is not abandoning you forever but *will be back* after the break is important to internalize and will help you tolerate the separation.

Don't Distract: Go Into Your Feelings

After you have disengaged, however, you will need to prevent yourself from distracting. Tom distracts with some shop project. Sanjit will go to work. Sandy goes shopping. Don't distract. Instead, go into a separate room, pull the shades, and lie down on your back on the bed.

Let's review what I suggested you begin doing way back in Chapter 4:

Breathe as deeply as you can and, on the exhalations, *let your sounds and words out as big as the feelings are.* You might rage and pound, or sob and curl up, or go rigid with fear (Keep saying, "I'm mad!" or "I'm scared!" or whatever the right words or sounds are for you.) Try different expressions of sound and movement until you find what's right for this feeling.

Once you ride through the first wave of feeling, you'll find yourself resting and possibly feeling quite peaceful. Do not jump up. Wait, and breathe, until the feelings return. Ride through at least three waves. Keep asking yourself, "When have I felt this feeling before?" Allow yourself to go as far back in time as you can. You may find memories you didn't know you had. Simply feel how you feel about them.

One part of your mind will say things like, "I feel like an idiot doing this!" "This is too hard!" or even "It's impossible for anyone to remember this far back!" I encourage you to move out of judgment at this point and into feeling—the judgment game is simply a way the mind distracts us from feeling. Just keep bringing yourself back to the feeling.

In time, as you go over and over certain big feelings, you will eventually separate what's true for you from what might be a symbolization of the feeling. Be patient. Give yourself plenty of time.

There will be one part of your brain that will try all sorts of maneuvers to keep you away from feeling anything. For instance, when Tom weaned himself off the shop and tried to get to feelings that seemed huge when he was face to face with Sandy, he found himself lying on his bed without a clue what he was doing there. He suddenly didn't feel upset at all. He just felt sleepy. But as soon as he got up and walked out, all it took was seeing Sandy's icy glare to re-trigger him. Because most of us are so practiced at stuffing feelings, it will take some time to get comfortable with allowing them to move up into consciousness. If you need assistance with this process, don't hesitate to do some work with a feeling-based therapist. (See "How to find a good therapist" in the Appendix.)

Most feelings in relationships are archaic

Most of the feelings that come up in our primary relationships are archaic, by which I mean old feelings from childhood or former relationships. There is almost always a "trigger" in the present that plunges us into a swirl of old feelings—and we usually fail to recognize that the feelings are archaic and blame them on the present relationship ("I wasn't like this until I got into this relationship with you!"). As long as our archaic feelings remain frozen and stuffed in the deep freeze, they will leak out poison into our present relationship. If we want to maintain a vivid relationship we *must* feel through the old feelings. Otherwise we will either part company or end up as emotionally distant roommates.

The benefit of the fact that the challenges that arise in our present love will trigger old feelings is that the archaic feelings are then immediately available. We don't have to spelunk down into the caverns of the past to find them. They leap right into the middle of the living room. And bedroom. This ubiquity of old feelings permeating our present can be quite upsetting. I certainly don't blame people for hating the experience and wanting to escape.

If in fact we are not biologically programmed for long-term monogamy and then have to deal with this whole cargo container of archaic feelings, I can understand that a new relationship or a solo trip to Antarctica can seem quite alluring.

There is at least one major downside to the attitude of "when the going gets tough, the tough get going—out the door": The golden opportunity to work through the archaic feelings is avoided and postponed. Archaic feelings don't go away, they just head back into the freezer for another term of hibernation. From there they will find other, usually more dramatic, ways of attempting to get our attention so we will finally heal them. Believe me, it is quite possible for someone to change him or herself from a salmon swimming upstream or a bellowing tyrannosaurus into a human being who can thrive within a relationship that goes the distance.

The Unconscious

Many of our archaic feelings are unconscious. That just means that, while they are present, we're not aware of them. The advantage of this function of the mind is that our circuits aren't constantly overloaded and throwing off sparks. However, that doesn't mean our unconscious feelings are not influencing us.

Sanjit had a lunch date with a friend who forgot about it and left him waiting in the restaurant. When he called her, she apologized profusely. They set another date, which she also forgot. She felt really terrible and promised to make the next one on Wednesday, even offering to pay the bill. Though Sanjit was frustrated and a little hurt, he was polite and said that was fine.

On Wednesday he was busy with a number of things and was shocked to find that he had missed the lunch date. He felt embarrassed and called to apologize, but after hanging up he noticed that there was some part of him that was tickled that he got her back.

The idea that some part of us isn't under our conscious control challenges most Americans. Even though Freud elucidated the discovery of the unconscious over a hundred years ago, proving its existence in brilliant ways,[20] most Americans, especially in contrast to most Europeans, are still loathe to accept that there can be an unknown part of ourselves that has at least as strong an influence over our behavior as the conscious part. And though modern neuroscience also demonstrates the existence of an unconscious portion of the mind, I find that many clients are initially as skeptical as I once was that some part of us can be out of conscious control.

• • •

The Sufis are the mystical, woman- and wine-appreciating branch of Islam. They have a long tradition of teaching psycho-spiritual truths through stories. The following one illustrates the problem of ignoring the unconscious part of ourselves. Nasruddin, who is a mullah who likes his wine, is stumbling home from the pub when he comes upon a man on all fours searching for something beneath a streetlight.

---

20 See, for instance, *A General Introduction to Pscyhoanalysis* (1935), which is based on a series of lectures Freud gave at the University of Vienna 1915-1917. The lucidity of his thought process is remarkable.

"Friend!" says Nasruddin. "What are you doing?"

"I dropped my house keys and I can't get in my house," the man says, somewhat despondently, for he's been at it for quite a while.

"Friend!" says Nasruddin. "Calm yourself! For I, Nasruddin, will help you find your keys."

And Nasruddin gets down on all fours and begins looking for the missing keys. Back and forth he crawls, on hands and knees, under the streetlight.

But after an hour of doing so, when they are still not finding even a hint of the keys—and Nasruddin is beginning to sober up from his exertions—he turns to his companion with a pertinent question.

"Excuse me, friend," he says, "but are you sure you dropped your keys here, under the streetlight?"

"Why no," the man says. "I dropped them over there—" and he points off into the darkness far from the streetlight.

"Well, my friend," says Nasruddin, reasonably, "if you dropped them over *there*, in the dark, why are we looking for them *here*?"

"Because," the man says, also reasonably, "it's easier to see here under the light."

• • •

Obviously it is sometimes right to search under the streetlight, when that is where we know the keys to be. However, too many people, like the unnamed householder in the story, keep searching in the light when they know the keys to the psyche are not there. But it's harder and scarier to leave the streetlight and search in the dark. Nonetheless, most of what is truly important to our lives is over there, in the darkness of the unconscious.

If you are doubtful about the existence of the unconscious, please take some time to do your own research. [An enjoyable way to begin, after reading the Wikipedia entry, of course, might be Freud's

The Joke and Its Relation to the Unconscious (1905)]. Meanwhile, if we take as a theoretical given that much of our behavior, including our mate selection and what gets triggered in relationship, has a potent unconscious element, it will help us be more compassionate toward our mates and ourselves.

Doing so gives us a powerful perspective that really helps us move through the issues that will come up in relationship. When we get triggered, rather than jumping into it with our partner or heading for the door, we can recognize that archaic feelings have just been awakened in the dark and celebrate that we now have a chance to feel them through and release them. As we do so we make the unconscious conscious. It's as if Nasruddin realizes he has a powerful flashlight in his caftan and turns it on to explore the darkness.

This process of making the unconscious conscious is not an easy one and can sometimes be scary. It is helpful to have a competent feeling therapist assisting you along the path, assuring you that you are not crazy to be experiencing what you are and guiding you away from the pitfalls of denial and delusion.

But working with a therapist doesn't mean that the job isn't totally your own. Your therapist is just a hired guide. You have to make the journey. Most therapists schedule you for an hour or two a week. I would encourage you to journey into feeling on your own every day. Your quest is no less than freeing your soul from the prison of your past. There is nothing you can do that is more significant—for you, your partner, the human race, and the planet.

Become the change you would like to see in the world.

Make the darkness conscious

Our foremost job in relationships—and perhaps in life—is to shine the light of consciousness into the dark parts of the psyche. This process takes courage because most of us are uneasy about or ashamed of our darker parts. Please remember that as a small child you were quite accepting of those parts, even the most socially unacceptable, until you were taught otherwise. One client told me how he used to reach inside his diapers and paint the wall above his crib. In fact, many people who go on to become artists used that same first handy medium. My client reports that his parents were quite unappreciative of these masterpieces.

Everyone defecates. It is a universal human activity which, as I tell my backpackers as we head out into the wilderness on a yearly quest, is one of the primary gifts that we can give back to Mother Earth to help plants grow. Yet we have been conditioned to see our defecation as something disgusting and shameful, to be done only in strictest privacy. We then tend to have problems in this area, as a visit to your local pharmacy, with its racks of remedies to treat such issues, will make evident. The curse of hemorrhoids, epidemic in Western culture with its fancy toilets and straining to finish quickly, is largely absent among so-called "primitives," who tend to squat and to be somewhat more accepting of the call of nature.

This is but one example of how the natural being we are born as learns that some part of him or her is disgusting and shameful. You can think of several other parts of yourself that you were taught were unacceptable. Some people are even taught that it is unacceptable to feel good about themselves or to "brag" by saying they feel good about themselves.

The task for us is to become conscious of how much of ourselves was locked away in the dark dungeon during our early years, to have a good look at it, and to decide, *for ourselves*, how we want to feel about it and whether we want to reprogram ourselves. For instance, you might well decide that you will continue to close the bathroom door, thank you, but that you will now give yourself permission to take your time with the process. The point is that it's now *you* who is in charge rather than some caregiver who doesn't give you a choice.

As with birth, the way out is through. By following our feelings we can go back to the points at which we were bent from our natural inclinations, re-experience those usually painful twistings of our natural selves, give the brain time to change itself, and decide who we want to be in the present and future. In short, we can write our own scripts for our lives, rather than accepting blindly the scripts handed to us by those who programmed us. As we do so, we will live our lives and our relationships with greater reality and passion.

Is it the Devil?

I want to give you an example of courage in facing the darkness and persevering in feeling through a horrendous archaic experience that had been frozen out of consciousness. Although few of you reading this book will have such horrifying feelings, it's best to be prepared.

One of my first clients during my training in primal therapy was a young woman who liked the room we worked in to be absolutely dark. Pitch black. She preferred the windowless room in the basement of the Center. She was readily expressive and was soon screaming in terror. She screamed that Satan was coming into the room to kill her and take possession of her soul.

Now, while I don't even believe in Satan as an actual entity (though I do believe in the presence of Evil, as this story will demonstrate), her terror was contagious and, in the complete darkness, I couldn't be absolutely sure Satan *didn't* exist. I kept my back to the wall, ready for anything, and simply held the space for her feelings. Her experience of the Devil repeated itself several times per session for several sessions. Not having seen any sign of the Evil One myself, I was growing somewhat less fearful.

One day, while she was resting between waves of feeling, I asked her what Satan looked like.

"He has an ugly red face!" she screamed, and was into another wave of terror.

During the next rest period, I asked again, "When you look at him, what do you see?"

"A red face," she said, "and—something white beneath it!" And she was off into another wave of deep feeling.

I had no idea what this meant. Gradually, as she looked and felt, felt and looked, in that total darkness, she saw that the whiteness beneath the red face was a *clerical collar*. She went on, through many sessions, to relive the rape that her priest-teacher had inflicted upon her when she was a small child. She relived coming home with bloody underpants and how her parents had refused to believe what had happened. Of course a *priest* wouldn't do such a thing.

It took her most of a year to get clear that what she had symbolized as Satan was really her priest. This happened long before such abuses within the Catholic Church had started coming out. It took her another year before she could bring herself to talk to her sisters about what she was now absolutely certain had happened to her. Her sisters confirmed that something similar had happened to them. They went to the Head of the School to speak to him about the fact that at least one of his teachers was a pedophile. They had no intention of getting compensation. They just wanted this priest away from children.

The Head listened to them, said he was sorry for their pain and would take care of it, and—as was so often the case when these horrific crimes began to be exposed—transferred the priest to another school.

I have often thought how appropriate a symbol her mind made up for this man. While I still have seen no evidence of Satan,

I certainly have seen a lot of evidence of Evil manifested by human beings. Some of it is as apparently mild as not believing a child.

For those who think such memories are made up or implanted by the therapist, I can only say two things: First, I am always scrupulous about following my clients rather than leading them. I think it is very important for people to come to their own truth. I do not need to inflate my ego by thinking I have more insight into a client than she does. And, second, in this specific case I hadn't a clue where her feelings about Satan were leading. I was as surprised as she was to find Satan becoming a Catholic priest. And even when she was sure that this particular priest had raped her, I suspended judgment: Perhaps this was yet another layer of symbolism. After all, previously she'd been certain it was Satan. When she was honestly feeling through the fear, anger and disgust, however, experiencing a host of specific recollections (such as the color of her panties that day) and her certainty didn't change, I suspected she was right. The corroboration of her older sisters' own abuse made it seem even more likely that she had uncovered an objective truth for herself.

I don't want to get sidetracked here onto the difficulties of bringing such memories into court, which seems to me a completely separate issue. I would simply assert that telling people that they cannot possibly retrieve from frozen memory something that happened to them is to add a scurrilous insult to the horrific injury. Let me state as clearly as I can: I *know*, not only from this case but from many others, that painful memories can be repressed and then later retrieved. I have witnessed at least one originating in front of me. But don't take my word for it. As you stay with your feelings, you will find this out to be true in your own experience.

Give yourself time to make sense of your feelings

Don't let the Observer in you rush to judgment. When the mind is traumatized, it reacts by protecting itself. It can freeze the memory out of consciousness. It can disguise the actuality as a symbol. It has many clever tricks. Give yourself time to peel the apple until you get to the core.

When you first enter into the memories that feelings will bring back for you, it is probable that sometimes they will not be "true" in the sense of actual reality. They might be symbolic: A real priest becomes Satan. You will need to go over them several times to sort out what is true for you.

And what is truly important is not some endless debate about whose reality is better but what you know to be true for you. The power of the *felt truth* is that it will set us free from the ghosts of the past. There is great wisdom in the old saying, "You shall know the truth and the truth shall set you free."

My client who discovered that Satan was really a priest freed herself from an unconscionable sexual wounding and a lifetime of nearly constant anxiety. She was able to go on to lead a relatively full and happy life. She achieved that by facing her demons. In her case, quite literally. For her to do that required tremendous courage, of which I am still in awe. Though the fact that the rapist priest wasn't put out of the teaching business is tragic, my client feels good that she found her voice and spoke her truth. She is free, even if that priest, if he's still alive, will never be.

That is the central purpose of doing the hard work of feeling our old feelings through to their primal sources: To set ourselves free to be the loving people that we are at core. Yes, it is fascinating to discover that we can access memories we didn't know we still had. It is even interesting—if sad—to see how they have bent us from our original loving nature. But what's best of all is that we can now love and be loved in a relationship that is safe and real.

Not all of you reading this will recover such dramatic memories. Your own might seem quite banal at first, like the man who realized he was deeply hurt that his parents gave his much younger sister a watch on the same Christmas that he got his, after years of telling him he wasn't old enough yet. What makes such incidents significant to us is the amount of feeling they have for us and how they can contaminate our present relating. This man chose to marry a woman who thought it would be a lovely idea for both of them to get the identical gift each Christmas they were together. For their first she suggested new Rolexes. You can imagine his reaction.

The Love Letter

After you've plumbed the depths of your archaic feelings, you will find that your mind is very clear. It's as if the right brain, having been attended to, can sit back down and let the left brain come forward. Often, having flushed out your feelings on your own, you will find yourself content, needing nothing from your partner. You might want to give them a succinct report of what the sound and fury in the bedroom signified. For example, "I got really triggered when Sandy was so affectionate with you. Seeing that brought up my old fears of abandonment, but I know you won't leave me. I'm fine now."

On the other hand, if you've gotten clear that there is something you wish from your partner that is specific and doable, ask for it. For instance, "I'd really appreciate you if you wouldn't let Sandy kiss you on the mouth."

For a larger issue you might find it helpful to shift gears and write a Love Letter. The Love Letter is a tool I've borrowed from

John Gray.[21] It's particularly helpful when you get stuck talking about an issue. You know, those discussions that go on past midnight until you're ready to take the blame for anything just to get some shuteye. By three a.m. I'll even admit that all of the horrors of the patriarchy for the past four millennia are my fault. Waterboarding would be superfluous with me.

Begin by writing a rough draft that's just for you. Start your sentences with the words "I am…" rather than "You are…." Go through each feeling: "I am mad that…, I am sad that…, I am afraid that…, I am glad that…." Reread what you've written. Finally, come to your basic wish: "I wish that…."

Once you have done this preparation, write a second letter, *the one you'd like to receive from your partner about this issue.* Address it to yourself, as if your partner was writing it. Mine often go something like this actual example:

Dear Belden,

I know you are hurting and angry that I … (fill in a *specific behavior* here, such as, "lost your manuscript.")

I am truly sorry for losing it and for triggering so much hurt and anger in you. I can really understand your being so upset. I'd be upset if you had lost something so important to me.

As an amend, I'd like to offer to see if I can retrieve it from your computer and reprint it for you.

I love you, Yashi

21 *Men Are From Mars, Women Are From Venus* (1992).

The Love Letter moves the issue into a different format (writing), which gives you the experience of processing your feelings through the tip of your pen. (Do it by hand.)

Next, in writing the letter to yourself *as if it came from the partner*, you get inside your partner a bit, which helps you be less self-centered. You can also get clear what, if anything, you would like from him or her. Be sure it is specific and doable.

When Yashi is the one having the feelings and she hands me a "Dear Yashi" letter (in which she is specifying what she would like to hear from me about her upset), I can usually simply rewrite the same words in my own handwriting and hand it back to her. I am amazed by how simple and doable her requests for an amend usually are. I always imagine she won't be content until I at least slay a dragon or two.

Using Amends

The idea of the *amend* is, I think, world-changing. It moves us away from the standard vengeance mentality ("I want to punish you for hurting me!") to what will actually work to heal the upset. Whipping the partner just creates new wounds. An amend usually creates good feelings.

An amend is appropriate when you know you did do the hurtful behavior your partner is reacting to. Notice that it begins with you not denying responsibility but accepting it. Not by blaming or demeaning yourself in any way, but by simply acknowledging, "Yes, I did that." You can then ask, "Is there any amend I could make that would dissolve your hurt feelings?" If the answer is No, you at least know where you stand. If Yes, hopefully it is something specific and doable.

In the example in my Love Letter above, the file for this book was once lost in the bowels of my computer after Yashi had been using it. She offered to attempt to retrieve it for me—and was able to do so. I went from feeling sick about losing a couple years of work to feeling immense gratitude toward her. And, yes, I now have a flash drive to back up my work.

Endnote

Understanding that most big feelings are archaic and unconscious won't fix things. In fact, in the heat of emotion, your overwhelmed left brain might not even remember the concept. But hopefully, on some occasions, you can say to yourself, "Wait a minute! I'm getting triggered here! But instead of going unconscious into my standard procedure [fighting, fleeing, freezing], let me try something new. I can feel these feelings through on my own rather than dramatizing them and acting them out in my relationship."

Once we accept ourselves and our partners as feeling beings, we revolutionize our relationships, for passion returns on the wings of feeling.

9: WORKING THROUGH FEELINGS WITH YOUR PARTNER

The way out is through.
–Anonymous

As you and your partner become more comfortable with your feelings, you can, if you wish, take the step of processing them together in the here and now. When both partners are able to do so, you create a powerful intimacy based upon total transparency. However, do not rush into this phase until you have a lot of experience feeling through on your own and always be prepared to bail out of an interaction that is becoming non-productive.

When you're ready to start sharing more feelings with you partner, without dumping them on him or her, I suggest you begin with the Volcano.

The Volcano

The Volcano is a technique that I've adapted from Fair Fight Training,[22] where they call it The Vesuvius. The purpose of the Volcano is to spew out lava so it's not seething in your belly. Use this at first *only with third party issues*, such as your frustration with your boss or the Congress of the United States. Ask your partner for her time: "Would you give me five minutes for a Volcano about my work?" (If she says it's not a good time, go off and do it on your own.) If she agrees, her job is to listen attentively, without saying a word. To monitor the time one of you can set the timer on the stove or a watch that has such a function. You now have the floor. Rant, rave, bitch and moan, jump up and down, express yourself. Feel silly acting like a little kid? Ham it up even more. When the buzzer sounds, thank your partner for listening. She then thanks you for getting your anger out in a healthy, non-violent way. Please note: Shouting or stamping are not violence, but some people are uncomfortable being around it. If you are one, give yourself the distance that you need to feel safe.

In addition to providing you with a marvelous aerobic workout, the Volcano serves as a pressure relief valve, burning off excess adrenaline before it can poison your mood or end up being dumped on those nearest and dearest. You'll have fun with it.

People with children will sometimes balk at this idea. "Won't we freak the kids out?" they ask. I encourage them to sit down with the children first and calmly explain that they are going to try out a new game *to get their mad out* in a healthy way that hurts no one. Tell them how it works, step by step. The structure is important because it acts as a container for the strong feelings. Invite them to ask for Volcanoes to get their own mad out.

---

22 See Bach & Wyden, *The Intimate Enemy: How to Fight Fair in Love and Marriage* (1968).

When the kids see and hear you two going through the steps of the Volcano, at the very least they will be witnesses (sometimes from a far away room) to parents who are dedicated to "getting their mad out" in a way that is non-violent. They will understand that feelings are normal and that we can create structures in which we can release them harmlessly. What an important message you are giving them by living it.

When I taught the Volcano to Melinda and Sanjit, at first he was a little apprehensive that it would be just more of the same from her. For her part, Melinda didn't want it to be time-limited. After I stressed that a time frame was crucial for the Listener, she somewhat reluctantly agreed to give it a try in my office. Here's an amended transcript:

Melinda: I'm furious with George Bush and would like ten minutes of your time for a Volcano.

Sanjit: OK. I'll set my watch to buzz in ten.

Melinda (standing up and beginning to pace around the room, stamping her feet and swinging her arms): Listen, *Shrub*! I've had it with you! First you lead us into a war with Iraq with lies about WMDs that aren't there, while you let Osama bin Laden escape in Bora Bora. Now you're *waterboarding* prisoners! That's *torture*, you idiot! You're violating the Geneva Convention and international law! (She continues in this vein, sometimes jumping up and down and bellowing. Finally she drops to her knees on the mat I have in my office, grabs a pillow, and begins striking it with both fists, really getting her back into it and yelling.) *Argh! I hate you, Shrub! Uh! Uh!*

Buzzer: *Bzzzz!*

Sanjit: Uh, that's ten minutes.

Melinda (pausing in mid-swing): Can I have another five?

(Sanjit looks at me.)

Me: It's up to you, Sanjit.

Sanjit: Go for it! Five more!

Melinda felt done after another two minutes. She put her hair that had shaken loose back into her ponytail and stood up. I was struck by the color and aliveness in her face and body.

"Thank you, Sanjit," she said.

"Thank you for getting it out so cleanly," he said. "You were beautiful. You still are."

I asked her to go look at her face in the mirror and say what she saw.

"Well, I do have some animation," she admitted. "But what's most important is I feel great. I feel like I could take on the Marines. And that's a huge load off. It won't be held in and then spilling off on Sanjit. I think I like this Volcano thing."

I suggested that Sanjit take a turn. Often, one person in a coupleship will become the designated feeler and expresser while the partner can sit back. I didn't want that to continue for Sanjit and Melinda. Primed by Melinda's outburst, Sanjit was able to piggyback on the same topic, perhaps less dramatically than Melinda but nonetheless with considerable passion.

When he was finished Melinda applauded, then leapt from her chair into his arms.

"Take me, you Wild Man!" she said, and they both laughed, but I have no doubt about what happened when they got home. People often feel sexy after they get their mad out. The centers for anger and sex are quite close together in the brain.

Sharing feelings in the moment

After you have each shared a few Volcanoes, check in to see how you each feel about being present with your partner's strong feelings about *you*. If that idea is frightening for you, give yourself more time to acclimate.

If you're both comfortable with it, or at least willing to give it a try, sit down and talk it over. What structures do you need to put in place to ensure a sense of safety? I suggest, in the following guidelines, that the Speaker lie down on the bed and stay in that "sacred space." The Listener knows he might hit the bed but not her. She will need to place herself as far away from him as she needs to be. She might wish to wear earplugs. (When I'm with a loud client I often stuff balled up tissue in my ears.) Come up with a mutual plan that helps you both feel safe.

If you are the Speaker, refrain from personal attacks, name-calling—all the ineffective speech patterns we covered in Chapter 4. Stick to sounds or sad/mad/glad/afraid and you'll do fine. It's okay to say, "I hate it when you ____________" and then fill in the blank with a description of specific behavior, such as, "...when you kiss Sandy back" or "...when you call my mother a bitch." But if at first you just stick to sounds it'll be easier for the Listener and you can remain right-brained rather than having to search for appropriate words.

If you're the Listener, do what you need to do to keep yourself feeling safe. That might change over the course of a session.

As with the Volcano, ask for a specific amount of time but not more than 50 minutes. The Listener will signal when there are about five minutes left. Once the session begins, here is a brief summary of the Speaker's important steps:

1) **Disengage**: Close your eyes to break any eyeball to eyeball connection.
2) **Flush** the feelings, giving yourself over to sound and movement.
3) When you've dumped the first wave of feeling and are resting, **ask** yourself, "When have I felt this way before?"
4) **Continue** this process until you reach the primal roots of the feeling.

Let's examine each step in turn:

1) **Disengage**: You are not in your partner's face, which is the usual way non-productive interaction happens. By requesting the time and lying down on your back on the bed you signal to both you and your partner that you have stopped interacting directly and are exploring old feelings. It is therefore much less threatening to her than if you are shouting into her face and waving a finger at her. It frees you up to be as expressive as you wish, knowing that you have created a "sacred space" to do so. If your partner is still terrified by what's happening, she needs to take care of herself—by leaving the room, if necessary.

2) **Flush** out your immediate feelings. Make a lot of noise and move your body. You are focusing, first, upon burning adrenaline. Pound on the bed with your hands or fists if you feel like it. If your feeling is grief, let yourself crumple and sob. If fear, shriek out "I'm afraid!" or just scream and let your body take you where it knows you'll need to go. You can trust your bodily wisdom. Don't stop with one round! Keep flushing for at least three.

3) **Ask** yourself when you've felt this way before. Do so when you've burnt off the first wave of feeling and are resting. Push yourself to stay with the feeling and go deeper. Did you feel this last week? In your last relationship? With your mother? With your father? When your uncle molested you? Some couples will agree not to leave the process until they have each made the archaic connection. Go to the next place your feelings take you and enter that scene as fully as you can. Use all your senses to get there, recollecting

smells, tastes, and touch as well as sounds and visuals. Give your brain time to download the data from frozen storage. Keep breathing! Let yourself express whatever sounds or words come to you. Allow your body to move as it wishes within your sacred space. If you feel embarrassed by the sounds and/or movements, express that too: "I'm embarrassed! I'm afraid you'll think I'm stupid!"

4) **Continue** alternating riding waves of feeling with rest periods until you come to clarity. As you go to the primal roots of your feeling, you will have a sense of connection, of having come to the place where the feeling originated. Hang out with and feel through that primal scene in its specifics until you feel drained of feeling. When you really hit bottom you will feel a sense of peace and you will know, absolutely, where this feeling began. *You will also notice that you have little or no antagonism toward your partner.* If there is something specific and doable that you wish from them, that will also be clear to you.

• • •

What you are doing is adapting the process of feeling-through that you have been doing by yourself (or with your therapist) to the witnessing presence of your partner. When you are the Listener in this situation, you need only take care of yourself and follow the principles of Attentive Awareness (Chapter 6). Most importantly, zip your lip. Do not say a word. If you need a task, simply visualize surrounding your partner with a warm, loving light. This is also a good time to observe your own feelings, which will often get triggered by what your partner is going through.

How one couple adapted this process

Taylor, who works hard as an elementary school teacher and is the primary breadwinner, has asked Pete to be in charge of getting the trash and recycling out of the kitchen and into the receptacles in the garage when they accumulate, either on his own or with help from their two children. Pete has agreed that he will accept this chore. His career as a computer consultant leaves him plenty of time to help around the household. He chauffeurs the children to school and extracurricular activities, one of which, baseball, he enthusiastically coaches. He reads to the kids at bedtime and tucks them in.

In addition to teaching, Taylor also does the shopping and most of the cooking and cleaning. She sees Pete's handling of the trash and recycling as an important contribution, a symbol of his willingness to help her out. But when he lets stuff pile up so that she has minimal counter space to prepare dinner, she gets miffed with him. Even when she reminds him to take out the trash, he "forgets." It has just happened once more and Taylor explodes.

"I'm tired of you being passive-aggressive about the trash!" she fumes, then catches herself at labeling. "I am *so angry*!" she shouts. "I need ten minutes to have my feelings!"

"Okay," Pete says, a bit tremulously.

She steps into the hall, pulls her tennis racket from the closet, and dashes into the living room, where she begins whacking the cushions on the couch with the racket. The resulting sound is deeply satisfying to her and she's also getting the dust out. With each whack she howls her frustration.

Pete's eyes have gotten quite large. He stands in the opening into the living room, wisely silent, observing his usually sweet-tempered spouse. He doesn't want to get too close to that tennis racket.

After about three minutes of this workout, Taylor pauses and leans on the racket, breathing hard. Pete doesn't say a thing. He knows that it's important to allow Taylor to have time and space to flush her feelings. After she catches her breath, Taylor goes back at it for another round of whacking and howling. When the kids come in to see what's going on, Pete tells them, "Mommy's getting her mad out." They watch for a moment and then go back to their homework. They've been prepared for this beforehand.

On her third time through, Taylor has to really push herself. She's grunting now rather than howling and her whacks are growing weaker. When she asks herself when she's felt this way before, she falls onto the couch, sobbing, as an image of her father discounting her feelings over her wish that he wouldn't tease her comes to her. For a moment she time-travels back to being a hurt little girl who just wanted her Daddy to love her. She can see the sly grin on his face, smell the Old Spice aftershave he used.

Even when she is crying pitifully, Pete doesn't say anything or move to comfort her. By prior agreement, Taylor will let him know when she wants him to comfort her. Till then, his doing so will only interrupt her flow of feelings. He sits on the floor with his back to the wall.

Taylor is quiet for some minutes. Finally she sits up, wiping away the tracks of the tears and looks at Pete.

"I apologize for calling you passive-aggressive. That's name-calling and analyzing. I'm sad when I do that. What I mean to say is that I'm angry that you haven't taken out the trash and recycling by the time you said you would. I have a need for you to keep your agreements with me."

Pete nods and mirrors back what she has just said to him: "You're sad that you called me passive-aggressive. You're angry that I didn't do my job on time. You have a need for me to keep my agreements."

"Yes. I got in touch with how frustrating it was for me when my father would keep teasing me after I'd told him I hated it. I felt so helpless. I feel that same helplessness when you stall me on the recycling and trash."

Pete also reflects this to Taylor. He waits a minute to see if there's more she wishes to say, then asks: "Is there more you want to say?"

"Just that I'd wish you'd keep your agreement with me without me having to nag or blow up."

"I can really understand that you want me to fulfill my agreements with you in a timely manner. I feel ashamed when I don't. I have a need to be a promise-keeper with you and it's mystifying to me when I don't do what I consciously intend to do. I'll work on this in my individual therapy to see what it's about. Thank you for getting your anger out on the couch rather than me or the kids. I'm going to take the trash and recycling out now."

"Thank you for being so present with me. Can we have a hug before you take the trash out?"

"Yeah, I'd like that."

Pete moves to the couch to sit beside her. They hug for a long time. Until their children come in, beaming to see that their parents have worked through the anger and hoping for dinner.

The rest of the story

When a coupleship has a flare-up like this one around the trash, each partner usually brings a raft of old feelings to the issue. While it may seem silly to some people that Taylor is making such a big deal out of so petty an issue, the worst thing anyone can say in such a moment is, "You're being ridiculous, making a mountain out of a molehill." Our feelings are never ridiculous; they simply are what they are. The seemingly petty details of our lives are, in fact, what are lives are composed of.

The details of our lives sometimes trigger big feelings. When that happens, we know that we are receiving what I call "A blast from the past." When we honor rather than discount our feelings, we open the door to processing old wounds that can poison our present relationships if we continually push them aside.

When Taylor allowed herself to be, as one part of her judges herself, "a hysterical woman," she moved a lot of held anger out of her body. By staying with her feelings and asking herself when she had felt this way before, she uncovered an important archaic component of her present frustration—her father's overriding of her requests that he stop teasing her. When Pete overrode her need to have him do his job in the time frame he'd agreed to, she got angry at her father's ghost as well as Pete. That piece wasn't conscious until she allowed herself to stay with her "hysterical" feelings. Having gotten that piece, she found that Pete's "forgetting" the trash bothered her less.

For his part Pete was truly stumped about why he couldn't seem to get the trash out on time. Consciously, he really wanted to do his share and help his wife out. He felt guilty that she carried so much of the burden of providing for and maintaining the family while he couldn't remember to do so small a task as moving the trash along.

The following day Pete asked Taylor if she'd "sit for him," their code phrase for this process. She said she would after she took the children to her parents' house for their weekend visit.

At their agreed upon time, Pete turned off the phones, pulled the blinds in the bedroom, and lay down on the bed. He began by talking about his guilt for not being able to get the recycling done on time, which led him to his guilt about not being a better provider for her and the kids. One part of Taylor wanted to interrupt him to say that she was perfectly happy with how much his consulting business brought in, but she wisely held her tongue.

Pete then got angry with himself. He pounded the bed and yelled at himself, "What's wrong with you, you idiot! Put a reminder on your iPhone! You're a Loser!" After a few rounds of this anger, he switched to respond to this Should-er part of his personality.

"Jeez! You're so hard on me. I'm doing the best I can. So I forgot the trash—what's the big deal?"

Suddenly, he began to sob. His body contorted.

"I'm sorry, Mommy! I didn't mean to!" he yelled, sobbing violently now, the quality of his voice changing to that of a little boy. Knowing that he is contacting archaic feelings, Taylor overrides her impulse to go to him and hold him.

Pete stayed with the old feelings for about half an hour. When he came back to the present, breathing deeply and peacefully, Taylor saw that his face looked years younger. After a few minutes of quiet, he cleared his throat.

"Mom was a control freak," he began, his voice deeper now, softer. "She had a thousand rules we had to follow. My older sister rebelled, and Mom beat her with her hairbrush. I mean really thrashed her. It scared the hell outa me. When I saw that, I decided to go stealth. I was a 'good boy' but I also would 'forget' to do what she wanted. She'd rage at me, call me a dumbass and a loser—just like I started out this session doing—but she seldom beat me. She bought my story that I had a poor memory. That's how I survived childhood. So when you, who takes care of me in so many ways, want me to do stuff like take over the trash and recycling, I go unconscious and act toward you as I did toward my mother."

He sat up on the side of the bed, facing Taylor.

"How am I going to get past this ineffective behavior?" he asked.

Even though this is a direct question appealing to her tendency to come up with the answers for others, Taylor is wise enough to hand the process back to him.

"What do you think would help you get there?" she asks.

"By doing what I just did," Pete says. "I need to feel it through. Just this piece I did today will make it easier for me to keep that agreement. And I like my Should-er's idea about programming a reminder on my iPhone. That will probably work now that I've felt through this piece."

He goes to her and hugs her.

"Thank you," he says.

Taking Responsibility for Ourselves and Our Ghosts

Around the trash issue, Pete was being stymied by the ghost of his mother and Taylor was being frustrated by the ghost of her father. In such situations, a couple will find that, until they exorcise these ghosts through deep feelings, they will keep repeating the same old dance. Any "rational" attempt to remedy the situation will get sabotaged, sooner or later, by the ghosts. For example, Pete's idea about setting up a reminder for himself might well work for awhile even if he hadn't done the feeling work, but you can bet your last dollar that after some time his iPhone would develop a glitch or his rebellion toward his Mommy surrogate would show up in some other area.

Once a couple understands that their relationship *will* trigger old feelings, not because they are bad or screwed up people but because all relationships do so, they can move past attempting to protect their own egos and get down to the work of confronting their ghosts. This understanding helps them move from seeing the partner as an adversary to seeing him or her as a helpmate on the path to good relating.

The most valuable tool you have in your toolbox is the capacity to take responsibility for and to feel through your feelings. Remember that no one else is responsible for your feelings—no one can "make" you mad, despite this misleading semantic structure in English. Xantippe couldn't make Socrates mad because he accepted her for who she was. While your partner can and will act as a triggering mechanism for your feelings, it's you who's getting mad or sad or scared. No one can even make you happy. If you can get happy around certain people, how wonderful. Since you are totally responsible for your feelings, you are the one who has the leverage to move them through or to welcome them in. Do not surrender this valuable right and see yourself as someone else's victim.

Remember that feelings, like energy, are not good or bad. They simply are. They are not actions. They are not forever. Like all energies, they dissipate over time unless they are dammed up. When made conscious, expressed, and heard, they dissipate faster. Learn what you can do to move through your big ol' feelings more and more efficiently. Life is too short to be stuck in the past.

Getting Into Feelings Simultaneously

When one partner is having feelings, it's quite likely that the other partner will get triggered, for feelings are contagious. Some couples agree beforehand together that if the Listener becomes overloaded with his own feelings, rather than leaving the room he will get down into his own process *at the same time.* To accommodate two people having feelings in the same room, it is helpful to have a second "sacred space"—a futon, a piece of foam, or several folded quilts—already laid out on the floor. If the Speaker has previously agreed to it, the former Listener abandons his post, drops into his own sacred space, and goes with the sounds and movements of his own process.

While it might seem that the original Speaker might find this distracting, often the opposite is the case: Having another person in the same room experiencing deep feelings can trigger deeper levels than one might get to on her own. Each partner can find themselves bouncing off of the other's stuff.

Some of these couples playfully call this format Scream Group.

In this format, such couples have come full circle to a new place. In their former incarnation they were both screaming *at* each other—and getting nowhere. Now they are blasting out their own pain in parallel teamwork, taking complete responsibility for it, and working together to feel it through so they can tame the ghosts of the past and be able to share a vivid loving relationship in the present.

This is the place the couples we worked with at The Primal Center in Berkeley came to. I should say that they had all had at least a year of individual and group feeling therapy and also been supervised in what we called Self-Help Group to be good Listeners for each other going through deep feelings. They also had therapeutic guidance in having their feelings simultaneously. They were the pioneer couples for the tools passed on to you in this book. A very high percentage of them are still together in honest, vivid relationships. I would like to honor them and their courage and hard work.

Because of what they were able to achieve, I have no hesitation in encouraging you to pick up these methodologies and make them your own. From time immemorial couples have been dealing with archaic feelings and the myriad challenges of relationship. You will also be able to. When you occasionally get to a stuck point, please get assistance from a competent feeling therapist. See the Appendix for the section on finding such a therapist.

• • •

When I ask couples who come to me for help where they think the problem lies, most of them tell me, "Communication," which is what we will turn to next. Notice, however, how much foundation we have built before getting there. In fact, one can learn all the communications skills in the world and still make a mess of relating when archaic feelings erupt. That's why we had to cover feelings first. If you can handle your feelings, you can get by with spotty communication skills. If you can't, communications alone won't help you much. But once you have some experience in handling feelings, particularly old feelings, and you then learn to be a skillful communicator, you are golden. You have both sides of your brain working together.

PART IV: COMPASSIONATE COMMUNICATION

Once you know what's going on inside and what you want, having distinguished that from some archaic unmet need, you are then ready to communicate that important information to your partner.

You will do so largely with spoken or written words. It is important to realize that the words you choose are clumsy signposts pointing toward a meaning that you *think* you grasp but about which you might be unclear. Your partner takes your string of those signposts and attempts to de-code them, using his or her internalized code-book of what those signposts mean to him or her—which are probably different from what they mean to you. Just because you have two speakers both using American English doesn't mean they'll readily understand one another. Let go of that expectation. Rather, remember the reality that 80% of the time you are likely to miscommunicate. Be compassionate toward yourself and your partner as you attempt this challenging and marvelous human activity.

In this section we'll look at some of the practicalities of human communication, verbal and non-verbal. I'll distinguish between what makes for effective as opposed to ineffective word choices. Finally, I'll give you a map for how to negotiate your way through conflicts in a way that will have both partners smiling.

10: EFFECTIVE VERBAL COMMUNICATION

It is in vain that we say what we see;
what we see never resides in what we say.
–Michel Foucault

The relationship in which I had the clearest communicational system was with my Chinese friend Mei-yu. Because her native language was Mandarin and mine English, and her English was only somewhat better than my Mandarin, we expected that we would have frequent snafus. When she approached me one day with the blender in hand, saying, "I will make some penis butter," I admit I had a momentary apprehension but finally deduced she wasn't intent on maiming me, having just mispronounced the English word for "peanut."

Such mistakes were the source of much hilarity for us and our friends. But precisely because we anticipated them, we gave one another the benefit of the doubt and used the Magic Mirror frequently to see whether we had understood. That is what I am suggesting that you do as well.

Two native speakers of the same language are more likely to make the opposite, and quite dangerous, assumption that they must be understanding one another. As we have seen, the probability of actual clear communication without using the Magic Mirror is about 20%. If you hold that fact in mind, it will help you tremendously in accepting the reality that verbal communication, for all its wondrous glories, is usually a very sketchy process.

Having this concept firmly in hand, the next step is to decide what is the purpose of your attempt to communicate.

What is the Purpose of My Communication?

Only sometimes will the answer be "To transmit vital information." A few other possibilities, if we are honest, are to manipulate, to hurt, to hear myself think, to attempt to impress, or to mitigate my discomfort with silence. It is beneficial to pause to ask yourself what you hope to achieve by speaking. At the very least you will become more aware of your motives. At best you will stop yourself from using words to attack or distract.

One of the reasons that we have looked extensively in the previous chapters at what is going on within us before considering communication is so we can better know ourselves and what is important to communicate and what not. We can then stop ourselves from using words to attack our partners and to focus instead on giving them important information about ourselves, such as who we are and what we would like in relating, which are the fundamental truths for us to communicate. So a first step is to be sure your meaning is clear to *you*.

Exercise

Take a minute or two to set this book aside and ask yourself what helps you reach clarity about what you want to communicate. To get you started thinking, I'll share the beginning of my list:

Taking time to experience my feelings.

Writing what I'm thinking/feeling.

Reading books and watching movies that get me thinking/feeling.

Hearing myself think out loud with a good listener.

Listening carefully to what significant others say to me.

Going on Vision Quest each year to simplify and to listen to myself.

Communicational Systems

Once you're as clear as you can be about what you wish to communicate and your purpose in communicating it, the next step is to be aware of the system inside which the communication takes place.

Communication happens—when it happens effectively—between two people,[23] each with a precise role. One person is the Speaker, the other the Listener. As you read this book, you are the Listener, I am the Speaker. Seldom are we that clear in speech, however.

What happens all too often is that there are two Speakers and no one listening.

---

23 In a lecture hall of 500, the speaker has many listeners, of course. However, each of them is engaged personally, one on one, with the speaker—or has fallen asleep—and the lecturer can only look at one person at a time.

It's as if there are two TV towers broadcasting at 10,000 kilowatts but nobody's home with a TV turned on. So the broadcasts are lost in space.

I actually had in my office one older couple, married for decades, who both spoke animatedly at the same time. When I managed to get them to stop for a moment, which wasn't easy, I asked them if they realized they were both talking simultaneously. They looked puzzled, looked at each other, and looked back at me as if I were crazy. It took some time to get them to grasp the fact of their mutual broadcasting. They'd been doing it for so long it was normal and invisible to them.

While most of us are less obvious about it, we're doing the same thing. Though we might not be speaking aloud when someone is speaking to us, our mind is racing, rehearsing how we're going to respond as soon as we can get a word in edgewise, or occupied with some other form of non-attention. What we are seldom doing is listening with heart.

It is extremely helpful, when you are attempting to communicate as a couple, to decide who is Speaking right now and who is therefore the Listener.

When one of you asks the other if this is a good time for them to hear you, you thereby consciously frame the context—and make effective communication much more likely. The one who requests the time is then the Speaker.

The Listener's job, as we have already detailed, is to be fully present and attentive to the Speaker. It is helpful if you, as Listener, can take a moment to shift from whatever your attention was on previously to coming back into touch, first with your body and heart, then with your partner. This process helps you listen with your whole body, not just your mind. This is the greatest gift you can give to your partner. What most people really, truly, deeply long for is to be understood.

Unlike my mutually-babbling couple, we now have one partner truly listening and the other knowing she is being attended to carefully and lovingly. Hopefully, she has asked for a specific period of time, such as five minutes, but if not she has the floor until she feels her communication is complete, or until the Listener needs a break.

We are seldom so formal in our culture. Instead we tend to trade one-liners, like two contestants in a tennis game batting the ball back and forth across the net. Dramatists from Sophocles on down have had a name for this form: stichomythia. Engaging in it, we can feel bright and witty. It is the backbone of all sitcoms.

However, it is not very effective for communication.

By contrast, in Native American cultures, whoever was speaking was listened to very carefully, whether or not he or she held the Talking Stick. When the Speaker stops talking, no one says anything for about one minute.

We seldom give anyone that kind of respectful silence. Notice how promptly we tend to pounce upon a Speaker's slightest pause to start in ourselves.

You might wish to select a Talking Stick for important relationship communications. It is an outward and visible symbol that helps remind both people of who is Speaker and who Listener. It needn't be an actual decorated stick—we sometimes use a wooden spoon from the kitchen—but if you make the effort to construct a special artifact with paint and feathers, it might help remind you of the sacredness of your communication.

Furthermore, you might want to see what happens when you don't jump in immediately when your partner has paused for a breath. If you have to reach out for the Stick, your partner can still gracefully maintain possession if she or he has more to say.

Only when the Stick changes possession do you now become the Speaker and your Partner, the former Speaker, now switches to heartfelt Listening mode. The exchange of the Stick helps both partners know that the roles have changed and helps them embody them.

The important thing is to become vividly conscious that (a) an important communication is happening and (b) who is in each role at any given moment.

Words Are Just Signposts

For much of human history, words seemed to possess magical properties. Some people actually died when cursed by a bard or wizard. Some still do in voodoo cultures. We can certainly understand that words have the power to wound deeply.

However, we need to take words down a peg.

I would point out that all words are abstractions. When I say "sugar" you probably think you know what I am talking about, though your mental image might be white and mine brown, or vice versa, and you might even taste sweetness on your tongue, but it will have no calories. You cannot eat my words. On a diet of words you would become quite thin.

The word "sugar" is merely a signpost pointing toward a meaning, as are all words.

I have an image in my head. I want to communicate it to you. I quickly scan for an appropriate word and come up with a coded abstraction in English: sugar.

Your ears, hopefully but not always (did you hear "sugar" or "salt"?), take in the vibrations on the air of that word with accuracy and neurons deliver it to the appropriate spot in the brain where you decode the word *within your own associations and experience.* Perhaps you are a diabetic who knows that sugar could kill him. Perhaps you think sugar is the root of all evil, not only rotting teeth but souls. Or perhaps you become warm and happy at the thought of sweetness.

In any case, how you associate to the word will be at least *somewhat* different from how I do—the communication is seldom perfect.

"Sugar" is a relatively specific substance. What happens when we start talking in grand abstractions about "God" or "love" or "fairness"? You can see the problem. The likelihood of a precise decoding becomes nearly impossible.

Yet most of us assume that once we've found a pretty good word or phrase that our partner will hear it and decode it in the same way we do. Such, I am sad to say, is not the case. Instead of assuming we're gaining understanding just because we're batting some words around, I suggest we assume the opposite: That we understand that words have very different meanings to different people. That we become more aware of the fact that even native speakers of the same dialect will often misunderstand one another. And that when we are able to actually achieve effective understanding we have accomplished a feat worth celebrating.

Use These Tools

1) Frame any important communication to lift it out of the flow of daily events. You can do so by saying, "I'd really appreciate it if you listen to me for ten minutes. Is now a good time?"

2) Be clear, through the use of a Talking Stick or otherwise, who is the Speaker and who the Listener.

3) As the Listener, take a moment to tune into your presence. Listen with your heart and body as well as your mind.

4) As the Speaker, speak Total Truth. (More on that soon.)

5) When you've finished Speaking, politely ask your Listener to mirror back to you what he or she thinks you are saying.

6) If she or he has gotten it to your satisfaction, thank him or her for their good attention and listening skills.

7) If not to your satisfaction, say what part they got and which you'd like to clarify further. Then ask for mirroring on that part.

8) If either of you becomes frustrated, take a break and come back to it at a specified future time. Be with your frustration. Ask yourself what you are expecting that is contrary to fact.

9) Keep coming back to it until you both agree you are in understanding.

If there are words you're not sure you are both using in the same way, play "Do You Mean…?" Ask your partner that question until you get at least *three* yeses. When you play this helpful game, often the Speaker will discover that she or he had meanings she or he wasn't even aware of during the initial statement.

Do You Mean…?

Let me give you a specific example of what I mean by "Do you mean…?"

(Whenever you are attempting to communicate with your partner, use specifics to demonstrate what you mean, as I am about to model now. Abstractions invariably lead to misunderstanding. We live our lives in specifics, not in abstractions.)

Okay, so let's imagine that someone says to me those magic words, "I love you."

So I can say, "Do you mean that you really like me?"
"Yes."
Okay, one yes. I feel good about being liked. But what does she have in mind?
"Do you mean you want to marry me?"
"No."
"Do you mean you want to bear my children?"
"No."
"Do you mean you want to go to bed with me?"
"No."
Boy, she thinks really differently than I do. Three noes in a row.
"Do you mean that you wish the best for me in life?"
"Yes."
"Do you mean that you will lend me money?"
"No."
"Do you mean that, in your eyes, I can do no wrong?"
"Definitely not!"
"Do you mean that you put me on a pedestal?"
"No."
"Do you mean that you'd like to get to know me better?"
"Yes."

Okay, I've finally come to three yeses, but notice how much more information I've gathered, for both of us, than if I'd stopped after the first yes. Usually we halt the query at the very first yes and then operate upon a paucity of information. Most statements carry more than one meaning. Make it a habit to discover some of the others.

"Love" is of course an abstract word. You can also play "Do You Mean...?" around quite specific words. For example:

"Can you pick up some bread from Briarpatch today?"
"You'd like me to bring home the bread for dinner?"

"Anytime. We won't need it until breakfast tomorrow."
"A single loaf?"
"Just one will do fine."
"Do you mean Alvarado Street sprouted wheat bread?"
"Yes! I love that bread."
"Will you also love me for doing you such good service?"
"Absolutely. You will be my knight in shining armor."
"Do you mean that when I bring home the bread you'll give me a big kiss?"
"Possibly. Depends on how I feel in the eternal now."

In this fanciful dialog I'm hoping you'll notice a couple things. One is that we can play "Do You Mean…?" lightly as well as seriously. The other is that we can play and have fun in our serious relationships. The fact that we are committed doesn't mean that we need be grim. But the fact that relationships can include play doesn't mean we should get sloppy with how we word something, as the next section will demonstrate.

The "I-Feel-You" Snafu

This snafu is a big pitfall that many people, including many therapists, tumble into. I've been ranting about it for 30 years but was often a lone voice in the wilderness until I found that Dr. Marshall Rosenberg had diagnosed the same problem.[24]

The problem is this: In the English language we can begin a sentence with the words "I feel…" and then go on to call someone a name, to label them, to attack them, to analyze them—to do just about anything *except* say how I feel. For instance:

24 See *Non-Violent Communication* (2003), pp. 41-43.

I feel you are angry.
I feel Jack is a yellow-bellied scum-sucking pig.
I feel like you don't know the first thing about women/men.

I call this semantic quagmire the I-Feel-You Snafu. However, it also covers statements with a *disguised* "you" such as:

I feel anger in the room.
I feel attacked.
I feel disrespected.

While there is no "you" stated in these examples, it is implied: You are angry, you are attacking me, you are disrespecting me. Each one is an *evaluative* statement. In each case note that the speaker's actual feelings are *hidden*.

Let's take the statement, "I feel you are angry."

How we might translate this statement into straight talk is, "I'm imagining that you are angry right now and I am getting scared." This new statement separates the story that's being constructed about the other ("I imagine you're angry") from the feeling statement ("I'm getting scared.)"

I am embarrassed when therapists fall into the same snafu:

I feel you don't get enough affection from your partner.
I feel a lot of fear in the room.
I feel as if he suffers from an oedipal complex.

Again, every statement is an evaluation, not a feeling. Nor is there any specific observation present. I am astounded at how often people, and therapists, get away with such twisted language—until I remember that it is how we've all grown up speaking in this culture.

• • •

Fortunately, there is a very simple antidote to this poison that I have come up with: Drop the word "feel" from your vocabulary. Ironically, when we say "I feel…" we usually don't make a feeling statement. However, if I drop "feel" or "feeling" and begin the sentence with "I am…" instead, I cannot fall into evaluation without torturing the mothertongue, as in:

I am you are angry.
I am you are not getting enough love from your mother.

Nevertheless, I can make quite lucid feeling statements:

I am mad.
I am sad.
I am glad.
I am afraid.

> Try, for two weeks, not to use the word "feel." Observe how that is for you. How do you feel about doing so? Do you find yourself tongue-tied?

The purpose to getting our semantics straight is to get the deeper structures straight, specifically to jolt us out of the pernicious cultural habit of evaluating others and to bring us back to observing who we are, inside. Dropping "feel" from one's vocabulary for a while expedites this movement. You will probably notice with frustration how often you have been using that word to encode messages that have little or nothing to do with what you are feeling within.

Why is it so important that we become more conscious of how we use words? The words we use and the way we use them determine, to a frightening extent, how we think, what we believe, and even how we perceive the world.[25]

The purpose of becoming more mindful of our use of words is to free us from the prisonhouse of our verbal acculturation and allow us to talk straight.

---

25 Whorf, B.L., *Language, Thought, and Reality* (Cambridge, Mass., 1956).

11: STRAIGHT TALK

The shortest distance between two points
is...a straight line.
–Euclid

Over the many years that I have been laboring to teach effective communication, both in my consulting room and in the college classroom, I kept thinking I should write a book focusing on the subject of communication itself. Then a client told me about Marshall Rosenberg's *Non-Violent Communication* (2003). Dr. Rosenberg has done us all a profound service by writing the book much better than I could have. And while there are one or two points where he and I disagree, I have no hesitation in recommending his book highly. As Jack Canfield says in a cover blurb, "Nonviolent Communication can change the world. More importantly, it can change your life."

Many of the principles that you will find in it you will remember having heard of in one context or another. What Dr. Rosenberg does cogently is to present them in lucid terms with engaging examples so that you can begin practicing them immediately.

In this chapter I will review what I think are the high points, but I strongly suggest that you purchase his book and read it with your marking pen in hand.

Here's a quote from the dust jacket that nails the essence of it:

> Most of us have been educated from birth to compete, judge, demand, and diagnose—to think and communicate in terms of what is "right" and "wrong" with people. At best, communicating and thinking this way can create misunderstanding and frustration. And still worse, it can lead to anger, depression, and even emotional or physical violence.

We can learn to speak to one another compassionately in ways that will minimize anger, depression, and violence. At the same time, we will stop injuring one another with the hurtful words that we have been using. Despite the ancient nursery rhyme about "sticks and stones," we all know that words from a loved one can sting like nothing else.

Good Communication Starts with Right Attitude

What follows will not help you if you are primarily interested in getting your own way at the expense of others or in having other people march to your drumbeat. That is *power over* others. That is violent communication.

Effective speech is founded upon compassionate non-violence, on a mutually-beneficial yoking together of two (or more) separate, equal, and individual *personal powers*. First, we are each personally powerful because we know what we feel and wish for and can put that into words with honest clarity. Second, we know that if what I want doesn't work for you, the outcome will be unsuccessful: If one of us loses we both lose.

Effective speech, therefore, is simply a tool to aid us in achieving joint agreement in a non-violent manner that leaves us both feeling good about the outcome. The most important step is getting clear prior to the communication what you wish for and need. The next is being mindful about the words you use, as we saw in the last chapter. In this chapter we will look at how to be mindful in how we frame the communication and to come from a place of compassion rather than the fear that I might not get what I need. What we are then manifesting is, "I am as committed to your happiness as I am to my own." That attitude underpins straight talk.

Avoid Ineffective Speech: Compassion Blockers

Despite what TV sitcoms might lead you to believe, straight talk is never about attacking someone. We've already examined this principle. I said, "You know what is ineffective; stop doing it." (Easier said than done, right? Keep working on it!) Remember, it's not just about changing the words you use, though that's a good start. Underlying all of those verbal patterns—of demands and commands, critical judgments and interpretation, name-calling and put-downs, dramatizing and avoiding—is an *evaluating* and *moralistic* mindset that does violence to you as well as to the listener. Rather than evaluate or be holier than thou, observe with compassion. What that means is that you separate your *observation* of your partner from any overt *evaluation*. You can become curious about who your partner is rather than invested in judging whether s/he is good or bad.

While this paradigm shift is easy to propose, it is challenging to accomplish. Part of the difficulty is the very way we frame thought in language. We tend to say "Violence is bad," rather than "I am afraid of violence and prefer win-win negotiation as a way to solve problems." We say "She talks too much," rather than "I get annoyed when she tells long stories about herself and our meetings run overtime." Note that in the evaluative statements there is a judgment but no indication of how the speaker feels about it. The moralistic stance puts one up on a protected pedestal where he or she can judge others without having to look inside and ask, "How do I feel in my body?" Asking how we feel inside involves a certain degree of vulnerability.

Therefore, an effective antidote to evaluating is to keep asking yourself (1) what is the *specific behavior* that I don't like and (2) how do I feel within (Sad? Mad? Glad? Afraid?) when I observe it. *You thereby shift your attention from imagining and then judging what's going on with the Other onto behavior and what you will come to know is going on within you.*

However, since this process is mostly unfamiliar to us and since our egos are usually invested in believing we are "better than," it is often difficult for people to make this shift. Let me give you a specific illustration.

An Intervention

On occasion a family will ask me to set up a session during which they hope to get through to one family member that his or her drug habit or alcoholism is painful to the rest of them. When the Smith family requested an intervention with their twenty-one year old son Blair, whom they agreed was a "stoner" and hard to talk to, I asked them to come in first without him so I could prepare them to talk straight.

Once I'd gotten all their names and their relationship to Blair sorted out (there was a grandmother who raised him for several years and an uncle who'd first turned Blair on to marijuana), I asked them what behavior Blair manifested that was painful for them.

"He's a stoner," his father said.

I pointed out that "stoner" was not a description of behavior but a judgmental label.

"What he means is," Blair's mother said, "is that he's a lazy bum."

"'Lazy bum' is another label," I said. "It doesn't say what he's doing, or not doing, that's painful to you."

"Boy," Grandma said, "you're asking us a really hard question."

After some more discussion, they were able to identify that what was most painful for them about Blair's behavior was that he hadn't paid his agreed-upon rent on the guest house he was living in on Grandma's property and they were afraid that if they held the line on collecting it he'd end up homeless and drift out of their lives.

When Blair joined us for the second session, which I had purposely set early in the day, hoping he'd be sober, he hugged everyone, myself included. His clothing reeked of marijuana. After I said that his family members had asked for this meeting because they wanted to talk with him, no one said anything for a long minute.

When I finally asked if anyone was going to say anything, his mother blurted out, "It's because you're a stoner and a lazy bum."

• • •

Even when the family members had spent an hour learning the differences between evaluating and observing—and coming up with a list of specific observations—in the heat of the moment they regressed to their customary behaviors of going silent and then evaluating. Telling someone he is a "lazy bum" is very likely to provoke a defensive reaction and it certainly did in Blair. However, when I helped them return to the list of specifics, Blair could hear their concerns about his behavior.

He was moved to tears. His uncle cried, too, saying that he felt awful for being the one to introduce him to pot.

"I didn't know you guys cared," Blair said. "I really want to break this habit."

When they told him they were willing to drive him to a rehabilitation center directly from my office for a program they would pay for, he seemed shocked, then said he'd swing by his "pad" to "pick up a few things." When Grandma handed him a suitcase, already packed with a few changes of clothing and his toiletries—but not his stash—he laughed, said "Busted!" and began hugging everyone again.

One lesson of this story is that it is hard to change behavior just through insight: Although the family grasped the concept, they reverted to silence and evaluation; Blair "got it" when they spoke of his behavior—and then promptly started planning how to take his stash with him. Give yourselves time to make the changes you each wish to make. Be compassionate rather than moralistic about that effort as well. Give your human brains time to re-route neurons. The brain can change itself—it just takes some time.

Exercise

This week, watch your mind as a cat might a mousehole for evaluative judgments. When you catch one, don't blame yourself, moralistically, for being evaluative. Just celebrate the catch—and notice you can now choose whether to speak that judgment, keep it quiet, or re-word it as an observation. For example, when I say, "I don't like Brussels sprouts" that is an observation. If I say, "If you like Brussels sprouts, you are weird," I am evaluating.

Assumptions Block Compassion

It is usual for couples to come into my office with rather fixed ideas about who each of them is. They tend to describe each other in general or global terms. Paul and Karin were such a couple. When I asked them about the issue they wanted to address, Paul said, "She's totally compulsive about cleanliness." Karin retorted "He's a big slob."

Part of my job is to help such a couple move from the general to the specific, and from moralistic evaluation to compassionate observation. This change is challenging at first, when each partner is usually hurting and angry and scared. Often we have to address how to move the feelings prior to being able to change cognitive concepts.

When one partner *knows* how the other person is ("compulsive" and "slob" are both moralistic labels atop an evaluation), I make the evaluation that the relationship is in trouble. Such labels diminish the humanity of the partner. Then, practicing what I preach, I take a deep breath and begin to observe more closely what each partner is actually doing and saying, as in the following excerpt:

Karin: "I need to have my house in order."

Paul: "No, you need to have the floor so clean you can eat off of it."

Me: "Are you contradicting her right now?"

Paul: "Yup, I guess I am."

From his response I can see that Paul is willing to accept some reality about what he is doing, which is a good sign. If he'd told me he wasn't contradicting her, I'd know I had some really hard work ahead of me. I suggest, rather than contradicting Karin, he mirror back to her what she's saying.

"But what if I don't believe her?" he asks.

"You can say, 'You're saying you need to have your house in order. Is that right?' *After* she knows you have heard her, then you can add, if you must, 'I find myself having trouble believing you.'"

This shifts him from the exterior argument with his partner to what's going on within him—*his* difficulty in believing that his partner speaks her truth about what she needs.

I gently restrain Paul from going off on the tangent about whether Karin knows what she needs and get him to ask Karin about what, specifically, having her "house in order" means to her.

"I'm glad you asked," Karin says, as if I hadn't prompted him. "I need to have a place for everything and everything back in its place, after it's been used. I don't want newspapers and your business files scattered all over the floor of the livingroom. I am *not* a germ-a-phobe, or whatever you want to call it—I don't need to sanitize the bathrooms and the kitchen counters more than once a week."

Paul seems surprised by this information, which I have him reflect to Karin so they both are sure he understands it. He then agrees that he likes to have a place for everything as well and proposes that he be able to use the guest bedroom for an office where he can spread out his business files. Karin agrees, on the condition that he'll be the one to pick it up without complaining when they're expecting guests.

"I'd be happy to," Paul says. "That way I can be in charge of how they'd ordered."

I point out that he also has a need for order, with his files.

As they discover what each of them needs, they find that, rather than being disdainful polar opposites, they actually share a need for order, though what that looks like is somewhat different for each. They move from assuming that they are at loggerheads to finding a way to meet both of their needs with compassionate understanding.

Dueling Observations

I think it is a very good sign when a couple can usually agree on a simple observation, such as that the sky is blue today. There are couples who don't seem to have much shared reality. When I ask someone, as I did Paul, if he has just contradicted his partner, and he says, "No, I didn't!" I reckon it will be hard for him and me to find a shared reality. When couples then take the next step and argue about whose reality is "righter," there is a big obstacle to overcome before we can proceed. Those arguments tend to be both frustrating and endless.

An example that I often find a couple caught up in is who said or did what at a particular time. Karin maintains that Paul is the one who leaves the newspapers on the floor. Paul stoutly insists he never does, that it is their son Kevin's failing. Karin firmly disagrees. And so on.

I suggest that they will never solve this mystery unless they rig up a hidden camera but that, instead, they can turn their good brain power in a more productive direction by asking how they can *solve* this problem *for the future.*

The answer comes to Paul like a lightning bolt.

"Let's drop the daily paper," he suggests. "I never have time to read it anyway. The weekly news mag is all we need."

Karin agrees. The problem is solved.

• • •

If you separate observation from evaluation, you are much more likely to achieve effective communication that will lead to a shared reality. For instance, if you say, "I don't see the milk. Did you buy us some today?" you are more likely to get a helpful response than if you say, "You never remember to buy the milk!"

Focus instead on what is happening within. You know it's true that you don't see the milk. Is it absolutely true that your partner "never" remembers? If not, you're lying—and will probably get a defensive reaction.

Beneath most of our communications as a couple, feelings are running like an underground river. Effective communication begins with knowing what we are feeling inside and being able to articulate those feelings and our core wishes to our partner.

Then my partner needs to be able to receive those feelings as information about me, not as an implied criticism of her, and to reflect them to me with her Magic Mirror. When my feeling self is received in this calm way, I know I am safe and I can relax and be myself. I can then speak total truth.

Speaking Total Truth

I cannot speak total truth about you. I can only speak total truth about myself. As soon as I start telling you who you are, even if I am accurate (and most people aren't, very), I am only going to hit on a partial truth.

For instance, I can say to you, "I sense that you are insecure."

You are, no doubt, amazed by my "psychic" abilities. In fact, many so-called "psychics" make their fortunes employing this technique. Any such relatively general statement contains a partial truth: We are *all* sometimes insecure. The larger question is: Why am I trying to tell you a "truth" about yourself? I may protest that I'm doing it for your own good or some such nonsense, but what's my real motivation? To persuade you of how insightful I am? To inflate my own ego by being "right"? To get money from you? To get you to change into who I want you to be? To make you feel less-than?

My first mentor in clinical psychology, Dr. Beatrice Pressley, used this example in my very first counseling class to demonstrate that, like psychics, therapists can say pretty much anything about a client and they will tend to be believed. They are, after all, the "expert" and the client has come seeking guidance. Bea went on to say that such analyses are bad therapy: Good therapy empowers the client to learn how to know herself, from within, rather than fostering dependency upon someone else to tell her who she is. We each have our deeper truth within us. What we might benefit from is guidance in how to access that truth ourselves.

In a couples' relationship, it is ineffective for one partner to assume the role of guru or psychic or therapist. For one thing, it unbalances the equality of their relationship, which will ultimately lead to resentment and rebellion down the road. For another, it tends to impede rather than foster the growth process.

When I describe external reality, including who you are, I need to put on my humble cap and to remember that I see the world through the filters of my language, culture and upbringing rather than as it is. I cannot therefore say, "The sky is blue" truthfully; I can only say, "I see a blue sky." If you see a red sky when I see it blue, I can then say, "Oh, you see a red sky," rather than arguing with you about whose perception is "right."

People really do *see* differently. A common example might be illustrated by my good friend Stephen Khamsi. When we were painting and decorating the first Primal Center on University Avenue in Berkeley, I kept noticing that our color combination choices were often different. Since he and I usually agreed readily on most things, I found this interesting and observed it to him.

"I'm surprised at how different our color choices are," I said.

"You do know I'm red-green colorblind, don't you?" he asked.

I hadn't known, but as I reviewed his choices of color combinations with this in mind, they made perfect sense to me.

How each of us sees the external world will be somewhat different. People in relationship waste a great deal of time attempting to persuade a partner that the sky isn't blue, it's cerulean, or some such absurdity. Another possibility is to enjoy your different perceptions and delight in being able to see out of two pairs of eyes, to hear with different ears, to taste—you remember the Brussels sprouts, don't you?

So, rather than informing others of *the way things are* I can more humbly assert *the way I see them*. Then I am speaking my truth, rather than attempting to coerce everyone to see the way I see.

Similarly, when I release my need to tell you who you are, which will never be totally true, and turn that job over to you, we advance our relationship exponentially.

When I say what I am experiencing within, I am speaking total truth. For instance, if I say, "You are insecure," you can—and hopefully will—argue with me. But when I say, "I am sometimes insecure when I go to a new country where I don't speak the language," I am speaking total truth, for I am the world's foremost expert on myself. You can be, too. Once you are, you free yourself from any dependency upon others to tell you who you are. You will then increasingly find your truth within.

In relationship, I suggest you speak only total truth. Why not start today?

> This week, see how successfully you can speak Total Truth.

Those Little White Lies

"But what if it's something that will hurt and upset my partner?" people usually ask at this point. We've already covered the ineffective you-statements and sarcasms that are most hurtful, so that's off the table. Now we're looking at I-am-statements, as in "I am lusting after someone other than you."

That's exactly what Linda said to Bert in their first couples' session. She'd made the appointment and, according to Bert, a good-natured young fellow, "dragged me along." When he heard her opening line, his face changed from smiles to a mass of frowns and he began hyperventilating. For just a moment I thought I might have to call 911.

Best to hide that kind of truth, right? Wrong. Linda had found herself becoming attracted to Bert's best male friend Joe. She had already discovered that attempting to contain the feeling just inflamed it and at the same time was creating a wall between her and Bert. She had made the therapy appointment to create a venue where she'd feel safe to take down the wall and get the feeling moving down the river.

After he recovered Bert was full of questions. In panic, people will often fall back on being hyper-rational, which in this case was a totally ineffective approach. I suggested that he take a few minutes to stamp around the room shouting, "I'm scared I'll lose you!" He looked at me as though I were nuts and then shrugged and gave it a try. At first he sounded angry. Many people cover their fear with anger. But after a few minutes he was sobbing, curled into one corner of the sofa, saying, "I don't want to lose you...."

Linda went to him and held him.

"I don't want to lose us, either, Bert," she whispered. "That's why I'm bringing this out. I need your help with this."

Most folks stop themselves from speaking an uncomfortable truth not because of how their partner will feel but because of how they themselves will feel when their partner gets upset. Linda had the courage to accept Bert's feelings. It helped that she wasn't consumed by guilt. She knew about the Love Cocktail and accepted that even well-bonded couples will face temptations.

Once his first wave of feeling had washed through, Bert was happy to become all business.

"How can I help?" he asked.

"By doing what you're doing," she said, "hearing me and having your feelings without blaming me. Then I'd like us to put our heads together and come up with a plan. I think I need to keep a distance from Joe for awhile."

Bert nodded slowly.

"If we told him," he said, "I'm sure he'd give us some space. But I have another idea. Remember how we always dreamed of having our honeymoon in Hawaii and couldn't afford it back then? Well, we can now. How about if we drop everything and take off for a month to Maui?"

"That," Linda said, smiling, "sounds like just what the doctor ordered."

• • •

Linda was both honest with and accepting of herself and able to speak total truth to Bert. He was able to recover from the initial defense of going up in his head, wanting to ferret out all the salacious details, and, with my help, to bring himself back to his feelings. That enabled him to get through his fear of abandonment and to his primary need of wanting to preserve the relationship. Linda could see how important she was to him, and he came to see that her telling him the hard truth came out of her wish to protect their love.

They had a wonderful belated honeymoon together on Maui. I got a postcard from them with a picture of the Haleakela caldera on one side and "We're in love again! Thanks for helping us blow out the magma!" on the other. When they returned, they decided that it wasn't a problem to have Joe in their life as he had been before. Bert knew he could trust Linda to tell him if that changed. He felt completely safe with her now.

Should I Tell My Partner Everything?

No, just everything you're uneasy about.

Obviously, we can't tell everything—"Right know I'm breathing in and thinking about the Giants winning the World Series and, breathing out and feeling a bubble of gas in my lower intestine...." What I need to tell is *anything I get scared of saying.*

Rather than babbling trivia and hiding what I'm uneasy about, I need to reverse that priority: Hold the trivia and share those deeper vulnerabilities.

By doing so, you create the opportunity to be loved in your entirety, warts and all.

Terrifying? You bet. Start small. Do one revelation at a time. See how it goes. If it's too scary, come in for couples' counseling so a compassionate therapist can help you both learn to normalize and accept these "dark" parts of yourselves. The path of intimate relationship leads us into and through our dark places. The treasures we seek are in the darkest caves, guarded by the swift dragons of fear. We bring them up into the light of love and find that they aren't really all that monstrous.

Think for a moment of how many pen pals of hardened criminals fall in love with the convicts. They know that this con is in for murdering his wife. And they still fall in love with him. Partly because he's so honest.

Billie and Sal were beginning to date while he was in the last throes of a contentious divorce. He was particularly furious one day at his soon to be ex's unscrupulous attempts to deprive him of his half value of the house. He'd come into the session and went down onto my foam mat, pounding with both fists and yelling obscenities, but what really terrified Billie was when he screamed, "I'll burn the damn house down!" Having gotten his anger out, he was feeling pretty good when he sat up—until he saw Billie's face. Her eyes were like saucers.

"Are you really going to burn the house down?" she asked.

Sal collapsed in laughter.

"Of course not," he said. "I was so mad I *felt* like doing that. But being able to run the fantasy and get the feeling out, I don't need to act on it. The house is quite safe."

Not knowing him really well yet, Billie wasn't quite sure—until time proved that Sal wasn't an arsonist. Gradually, she came to see that his bark was worse than his bite, that he might have all sorts of dark fantasies but that he usually acted pretty decently.

This is the essential difference between a feeling and an action. We all have dark feelings—including arson, violence, and murder.

I love the story about when the Rev. Billy Graham's wife was asked if she'd ever considered divorce.

She replied: "Divorce? Never. Murder? Lots of times."

When we can give these feelings the light of day, they will mitigate. When we push them down into the dungeon of the psyche and pretend we never feel that way, they grow bestial—and will find a way to bite us in the butt. They can come out straight or they *will* come out twisted.

"Here's some info about me"

A first step in effective speaking is to give our partners information about us. How do you feel about being the world's foremost expert on yourself? For some people it's uncomfortable to move out of the old role of being told who we are.

I know one woman, who shall remain nameless, who spent years going from guru to guru, seeking the answers to life's thorny questions. She got many. But they were never completely satisfying. Like so many, she was a Seeker rather than a Finder. Finally, she ran into a wise Sikh. When she asked, "O great master! Tell me what I should do to become enlightened!" he stroked his long beard and said, "You need to stop seeking wisdom outside yourself and find your truth within."

She was stunned by his brilliance.

"O great master!" she said. "You are so right! And what should I do after that?"

I am sad to say that this is a true story.

Human relationships are fraught with such complexities. Ultimately, as the wise Sikh said, you will need to stop seeking wisdom outside yourself and find the truth within. You will then be the foremost authority on yourself.

Then, share that information with your partner. Say "Here's something I'd like you to know about me. I do not like green eggs and ham. I do not like them in a box, I do not like them with a fox." Or words to that effect.

Until you can say "no" you cannot *know* yourself. Interesting homonyms, aren't they?

There is a wonderful children's book entitled *George and Martha* (1972). George and Martha are hippos. Martha brings George green pea soup which George, who doesn't like green pea soup, pours into his slipper under the table. When Martha catches him at this, she asks, non-judgmentally, if he doesn't like her soup.

George admits, blushingly, that he doesn't.

And Martha says she's glad he's told her because she doesn't like making it and has only been doing so for the last twenty years because she thought he liked it.

I cannot tell you how many couples keep up such a charade because neither of them is willing to say "No, I don't like this." This failure to communicate happens frequently in many couples' sexual relationship.

Please note that when I give you information about me it has nothing to do with who you are or your personal worth. George is not saying Martha is a terrible cook. Do not take such information personally. Hear it as a simple disclosure.

Once you've been able to say what you don't like, start saying what you do like. As in, "I love it when you touch me like *that*."

Once you can truly say "no," you can then truly say "yes."

If you withhold the *no* it's almost impossible to get to the *yes*.

Feeling Talk

Once you know what you like and don't like and can share that information with your partner in a non-judgmental manner, you can move on to doing what most men fear most: Sharing feelings.

You do so in the same way that you share likes and dislikes: "Here's some information about me."

If you avoid the "I-feel-you" snafu, you will be doing so without a hidden agenda. Remember to stick to "I am…mad/sad/glad/afraid" and you'll do fine.

Of course you have to hang out with a feeling long enough to label it with some accuracy. Do not let anyone push you into a premature observation by saying, "But how are you *feeling?*" It's fine to say, "I'm not sure yet. I'll get back to you when I know." If you only know that you're somewhat uncomfortable, say that. It's a good generic stop-gap measure: "At the moment, I'm aware of being uncomfortable, but I'll update you when I get any clearer."

Guys tend to get terrified of the feeling question because we haven't had much practice in paying attention to and then labeling our feelings. In fact, just the opposite: As boys we're told we shouldn't cry or be scared and that one day we'll have to be soldiers to protect our country and get shot at by people trying to kill us. But we shouldn't be scared of that, either. So we learn to numb out our feelings and "man up."

Consequently, for most men, it's less frightening to be shot at than for our significant other to be angry at us for not knowing how we're feeling. We get scared we're going to give the wrong answer and she will scorn us. But we have the same feelings as everyone else and can learn to label them. Be compassionate for your American acculturation and remember to thank a vet. When the Huns are at the gate, everyone prays there will be some heroes who can suppress their feelings long enough to protect us.

Gals tend to think they know exactly how they're feeling, and then make an I-feel-you interpretation that leads many guys to believe that to talk "feelings" they have to make similar interpretations, which a genuine part of us doesn't want to do. Be compassionate for all those little girls raised to say "I feel you..." and to believe they're just saying how they feel. They, too, are products of their acculturation.

We can learn a lot from each other. And of course this is a sexist oversimplification. There are plenty of women who repress their feelings and plenty of men who start a lot of sentences with "I feel you...."

Let me give a couple of examples of when it's important to acknowledge feelings. Begin with positives—everyone likes to hear positives:

"I really like the way you kiss me softly."
"When you smile at me like that, I get happy."
"I love it when you wash the dishes."

Interestingly, some people have trouble getting positives to come out of their mouths. If you grew up hearing lots of positives, you probably find it easy to dish them out. If not, you'll have to retrain yourself. Remember, you need to give each loved one five a day. If it's hard for you, jot down each time you do it, with whom, and what you said. Tally up at the end of the day to count how many you did.

'Negative' Feelings

What about "negative" feelings? Well, the very fact that we consider some feelings *negative* says a lot about us as a culture, doesn't it? After all, we would call someone insane if he called blue eyes or black hair "negative."

There is no such thing as a negative feeling. Feelings just are. They do not injure us unless we repress them. It is the holding down the feeling that can injure the bodymind. For example, people who stuff their anger are much more likely to be afflicted by a variety of ailments, including ulcers, heart trouble, and cancer. But it is not the normal anger but the *repressing* of it that causes harm.

Take grief as another example. A loved one has died. You feel sad at your loss of their presence in your life. You may find yourself weeping.

All "negative," right? Wrong. Death is a part of life. So is our grief at losing a loved one. It reminds us of how precious loved ones are to us and how we need to stop taking them for granted. When we weep, our tears contain a chemical which, when retained in the body, causes depression.[26] Holding back your tears will bum you out. People really do feel better after they weep. The old wives' tale that you'll feel better after a good cry is in fact true.

Observe, if you will, how often we seek out "negative" feelings. Many people love a scary movie or a roller coaster ride. Others are drawn to the "good cry" over a sad novel. Still others seek out information that will get them angry enough to become motivated to work for political change.

The full range of feelings is a part of life and has many uses.

---

26 We are indebted to Dr. William Frey at the University of Wisconsin for this remarkable research, on a NIMH grant. Your tax dollars at work! See his *Crying: The Mystery of Tears* (1977).

What I am not talking about here is what we might call "victimology," in which someone gets stuck in playing the victim and focusing only upon his wounds and how unfair life is. For some, that can become a way of life. It is, of course, no more Total Truth than its contrary, the worldview of the Dr. Pangloss who believes this is the best of all possible worlds.

We will tend to feel a full range of changing emotions in our significant relationships. In fact, we feel them more poignantly in those relationships.

One strategy we can adopt is to suck it up and retire to our inner "cave," where we feel our feelings through in private. John Gray points out that many men will need to behave in that way.[27]

Of course our loved ones, observing us, will tend to think it's all about them. What they will imagine will be much worse than whatever I am feeling.

So it's a kindness to say something like:

"I'm sad about my mother dying and need to cave for awhile."
"I'm angry at my boss and need to think about how to handle him."
"I'm scared we won't have enough money to pay our taxes and need to come up with a plan."
"I'm annoyed with you right now and need to work through it."
"I'm uncomfortable and need to process my feelings."

These statements are not "negative"—they are true. Now your loved ones know what's going on and can organize around you. If they are wise, they will not push you to discuss your feelings until you am ready to do so. For example, they can reply:

"Thank you for telling me you're annoyed with me. If you want to talk about it with me, please let me know. Meanwhile, I'll give you some space."

---

27 *Men Are From Mars, Women Are From Venus* (1992).

What to Do when Your Partner's in the Cave

Some people cannot stand having a loved one upset, especially with them. They want to work it through *now*. That approach is usually counterproductive. If you are such a person (I was), you will need to learn to tolerate your own uncomfortable feelings and find something else to do while your loved one does what she or he needs to do to process feelings. At first, I had to leave the premises to avoid pushing my loved one to talk it out. I had to visit a friend, play a vigorous game of touch football, go to a movie, or even feel through my own reaction. Do what you need to do to take care of yourself and to give your partner space.

As the partner, be considerate, even when angry or disgusted. After saying how you feel and that you'll need some time, work it through as expeditiously as you can, knowing your significant other is probably on tenterhooks. If you can, give him or her a specific time:

"I'll be ready to talk about it tomorrow morning over coffee."

Despite the old aphorism about never going to bed mad, there are times when it's quite wise to sleep on an issue. When you have been partying, for instance. Postpone the discussion until you are both sober. Yashi and I have a simple rule: Any relationship issues will be discussed prior to the first sip of wine.

If you're sleeping on it, ask for a dream to help clarify your solution. You thereby enlist your unconscious to help you sort things. Just don't spin your "caving time" out endlessly. I would suggest getting to it within 24 hours if at all possible.

Feelings are messages from our deeper self to our conscious self. They are usually wise guides, seeking to make a course correction in our lives. When we pay attention to them, we find that, far from being negative, they are extremely helpful. In fact, they are what give our lives meaning and direction.

Wishes

What you wish for is the single most important thing you can communicate. Beneath our upsets is usually an unfulfilled wish. When you can identify and state the wish, your feelings will begin to change. Doing so is often an effective shortcut. We can cut to the chase by focusing on the wish.

For example, I can say, "Sweetheart, I wish you'd not interrupt my writing between 8 a.m. and 10 a.m."

What is important for me is to have two uninterrupted hours every day to focus on getting this book completed. I do not need to explain or complain.

The complaining might sound like, "Geez! When you come in to tell me my brother's on the phone I lose my train of thought!" All good I-statements, but she'll probably feel badly about having tried to do a good deed.

The explaining might sound like: "Look, any interruption derails me and it takes me hours or days to get back on track. It's not just you. I've been that way since I was a kid. I've always had to close the door to focus. I can't even have music on, as some people love to do. I need peace, quiet, and strong coffee." Again, all good I-statements, but likely to provoke counterpoints such as: "But you're happy to be interrupted when one of your children calls."

I think it was one of the Fords who lived by the motto, "Never complain and never explain." Not bad, as far as it goes.

Where we can really get off track is when we think we have to justify or rationalize or build a case for the fact that we feel as we do. That almost always leads to disputation, as others sense the holes in the argument and are tempted to challenge them. When they do, you rebut, already feeling misunderstood, and then they counter—and pretty soon you have extensive lawyering happening. Then the issue switches to who is going to present the better case.

The toughest couples I have ever worked with have been dueling attorneys. But they are just the epitome of what our educational system pushes—persuasive argumentation. However, it was no less than a Chief Justice of the Supreme Court, Charles Evans Hughes, who said, "Ninety percent of any decision is emotional. The rational part of us supplies the reasons for supporting our predilections."

You might think back for a moment to whether you can remember any examples of when your heart has been changed by argument. Okay, and how many of those were when you got into it with your partner?

I spent one entire summer futilely trying to persuade a 60 year-old former coal miner from West Virginia, who was doing pick and shovel work with me carving out footings for houses, that the world was not flat.

You don't need reasons for your feelings. They just are. Do you think you need to justify your eye color?

Once you accept your feelings and preferences, and those of your partner, as givens, like eye color, you can share them as interesting information rather than as topics to be debated. At the very least you will save yourselves an enormous amount of time. At best, you will find yourself moving toward compassionate acceptance.

People will often ask you to reasonably defend your feelings or preferences. It is a cultural illness. I will pass on to you the marvelous response that my former wife Gail came up with: "What reason can I give you that will make you happy to accept my feeling/ preference?"

Here are some examples:

"I'm annoyed that you ate my plums. I wish you wouldn't eat my special food."
"Why are you annoyed about that?"
"What reason can I give you that will make you happy that I'm annoyed with you?"

"I hate Brussels sprouts. I wish you wouldn't cook them for me."
"Why do you hate them?"
"What reason can I give you to get you to stop cooking them for me?"

"I wish you'd scratch my back."
"Why do you want me to scratch your back?"
"What reason could I give you that would turn you into an enthusiastic back scratcher?"

As you can see, what we really want is to have our wishes met, if possible. The why of our wishes and feelings is tangential and relatively unimportant. When people respect one another's feelings and preferences, without asking us to logically justify them, we will all get along better.

Shakespeare, as always, puts it concisely: "Reason not the need."

> Begin a practice of stating your wishes without needing to defend them and of accepting your partner's wishes without having to fully understand or agree with them. *The very fact that one of you wants something is now holy*. Note how much better you get along.

A Final Word

We've covered lot in this chapter. You will probably need to return to it several times to review a particular section as you gradually incorporate some of these practices into your daily speech patterns. Please be compassionate with yourself and your partner and do not become moralistic about following these protocols. Do not correct one another. No one does it perfectly.

I tell my clients that if they're getting a hit once in three times at bat they'll win the batting crown of professional baseball. When you have an opportunity to try a new behavior and you strike out or pop up, simply accept that as a professional baseball player does—as part of the game. You'll soon get another at-bat with the opportunity to hit one out of the park. When you do, it's fine to celebrate your success. Jump in the air. Hug your teammate.

By reversing our expectations from demanding of ourselves that we hit a homer every time we step up to the plate to knowing we'll probably go one for three or one for four on any given day, we align ourselves more closely to reality. As we do so, we become much happier people.

12: SUCCESSFUL NEGOTIATION: CONSTRUCTIVE CONFLICT

69% of the issues that cause conflict in any relationship are perpetual.[28]
–John Gottman

That scary statement comes from *The Seven Principles for Making Marriage Work* (1999) wherein Dr. Gottman reports that he has found, after twenty years of careful research in what he calls the "Love Lab," that active listening (what I call the Magic Mirror) alone doesn't work and that couples are doomed to have to live with over two-thirds of their issues never getting resolved. I agree with the first statement: Until you move the underlying feelings, even the potent Magic Mirror will fracture. However, once the feelings start moving, many more than one-third of your issues will

28. Gottman and Silver, *The Seven Principles for Making Marriage Work (1999)* p. 130.

resolve. My success rate, personally and with my couples in therapy, is around 85%.

Let's begin with the truism that conflict is unavoidable. *All* long-term intimate relationships will have conflict. And not just our romantic ones. Also our relationships with our families and children, our bosses and employees. Not to mention our relationships with ourselves. Conflict, however, is not the same as violence. In fact, what we will be learning in this chapter is how to turn conflicts from gut-churning horrors into pleasant creative ventures.

Next, let's acknowledge that we won't *always* be able to come to enthusiastic agreement about every issue. We certainly need to develop the skill of agreeing to disagree, though I can promise you a higher success rate than Gottman's. Gottman lacks knowledge of the potent tool of feeling-through. His approach to being flooded with feeling is to take a break, breathe deeply, and visualize a peaceful scene.[29] Occasionally, when the feelings are feeble, that will work.

We've already addressed the need to root out the archaic feelings that get in the way of our hearing each other so we can successfully solve problems. That is a *crucial* preliminary to successful negotiation. *Drain off the old feelings before you come to the table to negotiate and you won't find yourself hijacked by them.* There is no substitute for this step. Without it, any attempt to resolve conflict becomes a quagmire fraught with peril.

Once we've modified our expectations to this degree, I can make you two guarantees: If you use the tools in this book and agree, as a coupleship, to abide by the guidelines of Constructive Conflict, you will find elegant solutions to many more than a third of your issues. More importantly, you will discover that conflict can be constructive rather than destructive and that you can feel good after a conflict—closer and more intimate than before, with greater compassion for your partner and yourself.

---

29 Ibid., pp. 178-9.

Negotiation is a tool to be used when people are not yet in harmony to help bring them to an enthusiastic agreement. The overarching goal of Constructive Conflict is thus a peaceful harmony between you and your partner, not for you to gain success at his or her expense. Read over the following chapter together and agree that you will each follow the steps detailed here. Unless both partners are in enthusiastic agreement about doing so, the process has little chance of success.

The Fifth Way

Johan Galtung, a Norwegian pioneer in political conflict resolution, recognizes that every conflict has five potential resolutions:

1) I win. You lose.
2) You win. I lose.
3) Negative Transcendence: the problem is "solved" by avoiding it.
4) Compromise, in which each wins some by agreeing to lose a little.
5) Transcendence, which produces a resolution above and beyond the problem.

Conventional politics and traditional marriage counseling try to resolve issues through the fourth way, compromise, which, at best, leaves everyone feeling equally dissatisfied. Galtung calls his approach *the fifth way*. The intention of the fifth way is not to attempt to get two opposing polarities to meet in the middle but to *join forces* and to move forward *together* toward an *optimal* solution.

The effectiveness of his approach is perhaps most dramatically exemplified in his successful mediation of a 55-year old border dispute between Peru and Ecuador, which ended with no border at all.

Today the once-contested area is a thriving bi-national zone run by and for both countries, including a jointly administered nature park.[30]

In a nutshell, what you and your partner are going to learn how to do is not to avoid or compromise, or have a winner and a loser, but to join forces and work together to find optimal resolutions to your problems that transcend frustrated bickering.

One Simple Sentence

After you've done your preparatory work of feeling through whatever upset the issue triggers for you, you will be able to approach the negotiation in a cheerful and pleasant mood. (If you aren't yet cheerful, you have more prep work to do.) In addition, you will have a specific and doable wish pared down to a simple sentence. For example:

> *"When we're making love, I wish you'd look into my eyes."*
> *"I wish you'd cook half the family meals."*
> *"I'd really prefer not going with you to visit your family this weekend."*

You will note that the first two wishes are requests for a change in behavior on your partner's part. Whenever you ask for your partner to change his or her behavior, please do so with humble compassion and without expectation.

The third is saying what you would like for yourself. These wishes are usually easier to fulfill.

But don't just blurt out your wish! Create for it the sacred space that it, and you, deserve.

---

30 Alice Gavin, "Conflict Transformation in the Middle East: Dr. Johan Galtung on Confederation in Iraq and a Middle East Community for Israel/Palestine," *Peace Power* 2, no. 1, Winter 2006.

Creating a Sacred Space

Of course every moment is sacred. The problem is that we can become lost or distracted or exhausted in the flow of life. Here I am, sleep-deprived from a night up with one child with the croup and now changing a diaper on my youngest while thinking ahead to when I'll be able to get him in to see the doctor for the rash. You blurt out a wish—for instance, that I'll go with you to visit your mother Friday. I don't hear you properly or I say, "Yeah, okay," to something I haven't even considered carefully. Then, when I "forget" or say on Friday that I don't really want to go, you're angry with me.

The person who desires the negotiation is charged with setting it up *mindfully*. Ask for a specific amount of time on a specific day. State your agenda. For instance:

> *"Could I have ten minutes of your time tomorrow at 8 a.m. to discuss the family weekend?"*

You are thereby making a date with the potential to increase intimacy in your relationship. You are also giving your partner time to prepare his or her thoughts and feelings on the matter ahead of time, which is why you must state your agenda.

But what if your partner has a breakfast meeting with colleagues at 8 a.m.? Or knows that morning is not his best time? It is then up to your partner to make a *counterproposal*:

> *"Sorry, that won't work. How about at nine tonight, after the kids are in bed?"*

The Responder must give some thought to what will work for him or her. Will he be clear of distractions? Will she have sufficient energy at nine tonight? You want to work together to create the optimum environment for the negotiation.

If you agree to that time, fine. If not, continue making offers until you find a mutually convenient time within the next 24 hours.

If this process seems like a bit of a hassle, it is. Accept that, remembering that creating the sacred space is one of the most important tasks you can do in a negotiation. Remember also that it took several months prior to the Vietnam peace conference just to negotiate the shape of the table.

Set Up Your Ground Rules

Prior to all your new and successful negotiations, your very first negotiation must be to set up the ground rules for all your subsequent negotiations.

As my mammy Dora used to say, "I don't play baseball till I sees the diamond."

(Er, maybe she meant something else?)

Your ground rules will ultimately be your own, tailored to your individual needs. However, there are some universals that I would encourage you to consider:

1. *Safety first.* What does each of you need to feel safe in the negotiation? Do you need a certain amount of physical space between you? Do you need a support person or a therapist present? Are there certain words you would prefer not to hear? Would you like to begin with five minutes of silent meditation or listening to some calming music?

2. Both of you are to be *cheerful and pleasant*. If you cannot enter into the negotiation in that frame of mind, you haven't done your pre-negotiation work sufficiently. If one person gets out of sorts, that is a sign that you will need to take a

break so he or she can process the feelings. *Do not attempt to negotiate when one or both of you is upset.* How upset? For me, any point past 5 on the 10-point scale. Either partner who wishes to halt the proceedings says, "I need to stop." That wish must *always* be held sacred. To ignore that wish is the psychological equivalent of rape. Any break should be for at least 20 minutes.

3. If you reach an impasse, *take a break*. Set a time for the next round and don't discuss it further until then. Give your unconscious some time to work. When you do, you will find you come up with amazing solutions.

4. Your aim is an *optimal solution*, about which you will *both* feel enthusiastic. If you aren't both enthusiastic, it ain't optimal.

State Your Wish

Most people beat around the bush too much, thinking that such indirection or introduction will make their real request easier to hear. It won't. Nine times out of ten it will only aggravate your listener.

Instead, thank your partner for showing up for this negotiation. Show your gratitude and appreciation.

Then, state your wish, as simply and clearly as you can, hopefully in a single sentence. For instance:

"I wish we could put $200 a month into savings."
"I wish we could go out to eat Chinese food tonight."
"I wish you'd cook half of our family meals."

Use the Magic Mirror

Ideally, your partner will mirror back your wish to you. If not, ask that he or she do so. It is fundamentally important that you both know precisely what is being negotiated.

Once he or she has mirrored your wish, ask if they have any questions about it. In the last example above, I might want to know how you're measuring "half." Do you mean of 20 meals per week, if we go out for one? So, ten each? Do I make up my own menu or do we do so together? Who shops for the ingredients when? Who does the clean-up, the cook or the partner? What happens if I'm rushed and want to buy take-out instead? How often can I get away with that, if I'm using my own money? Can I hire a live-in French chef?

If you have clear answers to such questions, give them and get them mirrored. If not, say, "I'm not sure. That would have to be a sub-negotiation."

Quick Resolution

Frequently, when you've both done your pre-negotiation work, all that's needed is the statement of the wish and the mirroring. If your partner says, "Fine. I'm in enthusiastic agreement. Let's try alternating dinners for two weeks and then re-assess," you have concluded a successful negotiation. Write down what you have agreed to.

We tend to be relieved to achieve a quick agreement. Most people don't relish conflict. However, let me caution you about coming to too quick a resolution.

Always give the new behavior a couple of weeks or a month trial period and then *reassess* how it's working for both of you. Not only do you thereby give your unconscious needs time to show up, you also set a follow-up meeting to address any bugs in the program. Expect bugs in the program.

Notice also that part of what makes for a quick and easy resolution is the absence of any reasoning *why* I want you to cook half the time. As soon as I say that you should do this because you are a female chauvinist pig who has been exploiting me and all men like serfs, where is the discussion likely to head?

In healthy relationship I do not need to explain why I wish what I wish. The fact that I wish for it is *the* important information for my partner, who wishes to meet my wishes if she possibly can. Each partner is then dedicated to meeting as many of the other's wishes as possible and to meeting as many of his or her own as possible, as long as both partners are in enthusiastic agreement.

Will It Always Work?

If my partner's response is not an unequivocal "Yes!" then it must be either a "No" or a counterproposal.

In a healthy relationship, there are going to be few outright noes. However, if I am being asked to violate my integrity in some way, then I must say no, as Frank did just last week. Deirdre hated the neighbor's dog, who barked all day long while the neighbors were at work but she was home. Talks with them had failed to solve the problem. When she called Animal Control the person she complained to sighed and suggested, off the record, that she "Shoot, shovel, and shut up." When she asked Frank if he'd kill and bury the offending creature, Frank said he wasn't willing to do that.

Even if something doesn't violate your integrity, you might find that while you consciously want to fulfill your partner's wish you cannot manage to, as once happened to me. When I perform my ablutions in the mornings at the bathroom sink, I am not unlike a happy porpoise. I splash a lot of water around. One day, wearing an expensive silk dress, Yashi came in right after I'd left the bathroom to put on some lipstick. As she leaned up against the countertop, her dress got a nasty watermark. She came out into the bedroom, where I was dressing, and showed me the damage. I was aghast.

"I wish," she said, with some acerbity, "that henceforth after you finish your ablutions you'd take a hand towel and wipe the counter dry."

Every conscious part of me wanted to meet her request. But rather than simply agree, I wisely said:

"Gosh, I feel terrible about your dress. I really want to meet your request. Let me see how I do over the next two weeks and I'll get back to you."

Two weeks later, I got back to her. (Guys, you need to be promise keepers. If you say you'll get back to her in two weeks, immediately mark it down on your calendar. If you don't know *absolutely* that you can keep a promise, don't make the promise.)

I said: "Honey, I feel really embarrassed to tell you this, but I can't promise to wipe the counter every day. Over these two weeks I've only batted about .500."

Yashi was great. She said, "Well, I hear that you can't do it. I'm annoyed about that, but I'll find a way to work around it."

What a woman. (She's not *always* that wonderful.)

I tell this story to indicate that while this method is successful for us over 85% of the time, it is not perfect, even for so simple a request as Yashi was making. When two hard-headed people disagree on an issue of principle, they might not ever find common ground. In that case, they will have to split up or agree to disagree. When one finds he can't meet a simple request that he consciously would like to meet, he needs to be forthright about that fact—and learn to accept his limits and the power of the unconscious.

Interestingly, since that day fifteen years ago when Yashi released me from having to wipe the counter, I've missed doing so only once. What do you make of that? What does it tell you for your own negotiations?

The Counterproposal

When you can't or won't meet a wish your partner expresses, rather than a flat "No," I would suggest a counterproposal, if at all possible.

When Yashi and I were deciding if we were going to blend our families, one big issue was whether we would have a TV. Yashi and her children had watched a lot of TV; mine had never had one in the home. My wish was to not have one, at least until my children were much older.

Yashi said, "Well, that's going to be tough on my kids. I wonder if we can find a win/win solution around TV."

It happened that the place we were considering renting while we built our home had (a) a huge dish for TV reception and (b) a separate apartment over the garage, which we were going to use for our office.

"What if," Yashi went on, "we put my TV and VHS player [that's how long ago this was] out in the office. On Movie Night we can all go out there with a big bowl of popcorn and pop a tape in. After office hours, my kids would be able to go to the office and watch some TV."

Yashi's youngest child was then sixteen; mine were eleven and almost nine. Yashi thought that she could impress upon her children the necessity of keeping their TV access private.

I reflected her idea to her and said I needed time to think about it.

Having mirrored her counterproposal, I was in the position of deciding whether I was enthusiastic about trying this possibility or not.

In fact, I had some qualms. In general, I am opposed to subterfuge. I didn't like hiding the reality from my kids. And I rather suspected that they'd pretty quickly figure it out anyway.

Listen to Each Other Rather than Argue a Case

As you each come up with different possibilities, listen carefully to what the underlying need is: In the above example, I understood that Yashi was reluctant to deprive her children of an entertainment that had been a part of their lives. Yashi understood that I felt strongly about not exposing my kids to much TV and she wanted to understand that need better.

I told her that I had been raised without television because my parents wanted us to read and I felt I had benefitted from that decision. I wanted to pass on that legacy to my children. Second, I wanted to spare my kids the bombardment of both gratuitous violence and Madison Avenue. Third, I didn't want their sense of reality mediated by TV. Fourth, and perhaps most importantly, I wanted to be in a family that read and talked together rather than one that watched together.

Yashi listened to me carefully and reflected back to me my wishes. Rather than attempting to counter my wishes, she validated what she could. For instance, she said that she liked my vision of a family that read and talked together.

She listened to me with curiosity and compassion to understand better who I was and what my core needs might be. She was coming from a place of being willing to try her best to meet my needs. In the same way, I listened to her and validated her need not to thrust too many changes upon her children at once. They were already leaving their home town, changing schools, and leaving behind friends and easy access to their father. Any negotiation gives us such opportunities to more deeply understand and respect one another.

Neither of us made light of or poked fun at the other's wishes. Had she been a different person, she might have called me weird and out of touch with mainstream culture, attempting to shame me into capitulating to what she wanted. Similarly, I refrained from accusing her of being addicted to the plug-in drug.

What we avoided was *lawyering*, presenting a case that one person hopes will persuade the other to give up his wishes. In so doing one might, like a skillful attorney, try to punch holes in the other's case and build up her own. Note that thereby the "lawyer" is moving to the one-up position that implies, "I am much smarter than you and will overwhelm you with my clever arguments until you'll feel like a fool if you disagree." So you reluctantly agree, feeling a bit dazed, and then you will resent that you got steamrollered and later want to renegotiate.

The "lawyer" will then be outraged by your unfairness because, after all, you both agreed she was "right" and you went along with her conclusion. The discussion gets ever more complex.

Because our courts and our schools are organized around the argumentative style, we assume that this method must be effective. It is not. Business has long since moved away from it. Even the courts are trying to find another system that will work better, particularly in family law departments. The schools, however, are always the last institutions to change and are probably still teaching "argument" and "persuasion" in the touching faith that they actually work, in the face of all evidence to the contrary.

What can we do instead?

Say Who You Are and What You Wish For

You've read this before somewhere, right? Am I sounding like a broken record?

As we discussed how we'd relate around TV, Yashi and I got to know each other much better. Most importantly, we had a direct experience of the fact that both of us were respectful of the other's values and had no intention of riding roughshod over them to get what we wanted. We both understood that if one person loses, the relationship loses. We were committed to finding a fifth way that worked well for both of us.

Once I knew that Yashi was that kind of person, I felt safe. She had heard my wishes attentively, reflected them to me so that I knew she had heard me, and even validated the ones she resonated with. She never demeaned me in any way. I did my best to respond in kind.

She then proceeded to say that she had a need to minimize the considerable changes in her children's lives. She wanted them to be able to watch some limited amount of TV that did not contaminate my children.

I listened, reflected, and validated. I got to know more about her through that process: That she would say what she wanted and still try to find a fifth way. That she would protect her children's needs. That she would consider my children as well as her own.

We both respected one another's wishes, even when we disagreed about the intrinsic value of television.

We finally agreed to her counterproposal and her children got to go out to the office after our family reading hour while I was putting mine to bed. We also all enjoyed Movie Night together in the office, renting a tape and making popcorn and hot chocolate. I don't think my children ever knew, in the year and a half we lived there, that the box in the office had access to 50 channels. When we moved into our new house, it happened that it was located in a "black hole" that got no TV reception. Yashi's children didn't seem to mind and were soon out of the house anyway. When my kids had also moved on to college, I said to Yashi, "Now that the kids are all out, I'm totally open to seeing if we can get a dish or something. You know how I love to watch sports."

Yashi said, "No way. You've made me a convert. I really love not having a TV."

You will have noticed that a repeating theme throughout this book is compassionate tolerance of each other. Ask yourself, right now, to what extent you truly accept your partner as he or she is. If you don't, what do you need to do about that? Only when you are truly accepting can your partner feel safe to be fully who he or she is.

Take a Break

At several points in our negotiations, Yashi and I had to take breaks to process our feelings. That possibility is very important to keep in mind.

One pitfall in negotiation is that people can get "locked on" to the task and not prioritize, above anything else, the quality of the relationship. While we all like to get through to resolution as efficiently as possible, forcing a discussion when one or more of you is truly upset will not be helpful. A really important relationship skill is knowing when to take a break. Check your expectations: Do you expect that you must achieve an agreement right now?

If one of you realizes that someone is becoming upset, take a break—for twenty minutes or two hours or even a day. All you need do is to say:

> *"I'd like to take a break. Could we come back to this tomorrow at this time?"*

Do not argue why you think a break is going to be helpful. The fact that you wish it is what is most important.

A break can be helpful in several ways. First, it unplugs each of you from the growing intensity and gives you some time to feel through your feelings. Second, it gives your mind, both consciously and unconsciously, time to process. Third, it gives the deeper Self within you a chance to come up with an often surprising solution.

Let me say a bit more about this last point. The most creative part of us is not the thinking mind. In a survey of scientists and mathematicians, including Einstein, most agreed that their major discoveries or breakthroughs came in a sudden flash of insight when their mind was relatively still—in a dream or when sitting under an apple tree and being hit by a falling apple. We've been taught to believe that we must *effort* and push our thinking mind—to work it out with a pencil and paper like the constipated mathematician, to quote a terrible joke. Just the opposite is true. When we can take a break from the negotiation, a deeper and wiser part of our consciousness will go to work on the problem.

So take a break, give yourself some time to allow this process, and simply ask yourself, later, "Has my wish changed? Do I have any new suggestions?"

Then reconnect at the agreed upon time and place, state the new (or old) wish, and listen to your partner carefully—with mirroring.

Brainstorming

Still stuck? Brainstorm. Sit down with a paper and pencil (ha!) for a fixed period of time not to exceed 50 minutes. Each of you then throws out possible solutions, serious and funny. Jot each down *without evaluation*. You're just making a list and freeing the creative part of consciousness that is inhibited by evaluation.

When you run out of ideas, wait for another few minutes, being open for stragglers to appear. Play with funny ideas. Laugh. Have some fun.

I remember the wonderful experience of brainstorming I was privileged to have when the editors at the Berkeley Poets' Press were trying to find a better title for my first book of poetry back in 1976. I think my working title was something like *Confessions of a Male Chauvinist Piglet*, which they thought didn't do the poetry justice. We sat around a funkily comfortable living room in west Berkeley tossing out possibilities.

"I want to have a snake or snakes in the title," Marina said. "Something like *The Serpents of Eden*."

"And flowers," Charles said. "But not *Fowers of Evil*. That's been done. How about *Flowering Serpents?*"

"How about *Snake Blossoms?*" Bruce said—and we all laughed because it seemed both so weird and so right.

And that is the title they chose for my first published book.

Once you have a number of possibilities, move to the evaluative stage. Read through the list of ideas you've both come up with. Either of you may veto any idea *without explanation*. Simply say, "That won't work for me." Do **not** attempt to persuade a vetoer that he or she is mistaken.

If you come up with a possible solution, great. If not, take another break and come back to brainstorm again, fresh, the next day. Sleep, and dream, on it.

Repeat this process as long as needed. Enjoy laughter at the humorous suggestions.

Living Agreements

When you reach an agreement that you both like, write it down and initial it, so you are both clear what it is and you can refer back to it. Yashi and I keep an agreement book wherein we have a record of our important agreements from over two decades. When I review it I chuckle and feel fondly about the spaces we've navigated together successfully. I also am reminded of how fickle memory can be. ("Did I agree to *that*?")

A written record will also allow you to compute what percentage of your conflicts were negotiated successfully. I'd love to know your batting average.

Remember to give any agreement a trial period during which you test drive it and work out any bugs.

No agreement is ever set in stone. We scrapped the Wet Counter agreement after two weeks and the TV agreement when we moved. If either partner has a problem with an existing agreement, he or she can bring it up. The couple can then toss or re-negotiate that agreement. You have control over which agreements you wish to have in your lives. There is no reason to endure an agreement that isn't working for you.

Never simply ignore an existing agreement or veto it without discussion. If you want a change, say so.

We all change over time. As we do, we'll need to readapt our agreements to our changing selves and circumstances. You can look forward to a lifetime of enjoyable negotiations.

Summary

To conflict constructively, take the following steps:

1. Clear out your feelings, present and archaic, about the topic.
2. Make a mutually-convenient appointment for a specific amount of time.
3. Be clear about what you both need to feel safe in the negotiation.
4. State what you wish for—and ask to have your wish reflected.

5. Your partner enthusiastically agrees—or makes a counterproposal.
6. Reflect the counter and agree or make a counter to the counter.
7. Avoid lawyering.
8. If you cannot find a happy fifth way, take a break and allow your unconscious to work.
9. Return to the discussion. Use brainstorming.
10. Keep moving your feelings along as they arise.
11. Find an optimal solution you are both enthusiastic about. Write it down. Reassess in two weeks.
12. Celebrate!

AFTERWORD

If you've come this far, you're already a fur piece up that mountain path, toting an internal frame backpack chockablock with state-of-the-art equipment. Nevertheless, you are still the one who must put one foot in front of the other. There will be some steep climbs that you might imagine will kill you; they won't. You will survive this walkabout. There are some swamps to muck through. Sometimes you will misplace your new equipment, or your partner will. Expect the going to be tough at times. Expect that the challenges you face will force you to learn and grow.

As you go through the difficult times together and find that you can deal with the tears and fears, you will gradually build a relationship that you *know* is irreplaceable. You will come to a sense of safety and security that comes only from doing the hard work together. You will build, brick by brick, a home for a relationship that the Big Bad Wolf cannot blow down.

If you take only one concept away from this book, I would hope it would be the idea that our relationships are vehicles for accelerated psycho-spiritual growth. That concept will help you remember to be mindful of yourself and your partner as living and growing beings. When you hit a sticky patch—which you will, I can guarantee it—take a deep breath and ask yourself, "I wonder what it is I need to learn right now?"

It was the ancient Greeks who pointed out that knowledge comes through suffering.

Even at the darkest hours, please remember to be as kind as you can to your partner (and yourself). Remember that you are friends, not enemies. The real antagonists are the ghosts from the past. Working together, you can tame those ghosts and bring light to the darkness.

Remember that when these ghosts hijack the ship, which they will at times, the way out is through your feelings. Rather than avoiding feelings, hold them in the front of your mind and in your body. Allow yourself to weep. Grieve. Pound a punching bag. Shout, shout, get it all out. If you need assistance in doing so, hire a good feeling-based therapist. Go through the feelings to meet the ghosts that haunt us and transform them into wise mentors.

Be conscious of the words you speak, striving to become more compassionate. Give your partner the loving gift of attentive listening. Speak total truth. Negotiate differences toward a fifth way. Enjoy this marvelous human being you love. Have fun together.

You will co-create a very precious relationship in which you can be wholly yourself and fully loved. You will come to be able to love at a depth you never imagined possible. When you build such a structure together, you will know that it will survive any earthquake or tidal wave.

I would be honored to hear from you. What do you find helpful in this book? What was more difficult for you? Have I been clear enough? What have I left out, or overstated? What has happened in your relationship as a result of reading this book?

You can contact me at beldenjohnson@att. net or at The Center for Inner Visions at (530) 265-3737. I wish you well in your couples' journey.

APPENDIX: How to find a good therapist

When I want to find a therapist, the first consideration for me is whether I'm going to feel comfortable being freely expressive in their office. If the office isn't soundproofed and is next to the well baby clinic and over an insurance agent, I'm going to feel inhibited. An office that is off by itself and/or is well sound-proofed usually costs more, but I don't need more inhibition in my therapy than I have in my life.

But just because a therapist welcomes feelings doesn't necessarily mean that they are competent in other ways. The next step I take is to make sure that they are licensed. To be licensed, a therapist must accomplish a number of significant steps. For my licensure, for example, that of a Marriage and Family Therapist in California, I had to complete a master's degree *in the field.* The fact that I already had two other master's degrees didn't matter. I had to go back to college and earn the third. Next, I had to pass a general examination in psychological theory. Third, I had to be supervised by licensed therapists for 3,000 hours of practice.

Once licensed, I am now overseen by the California Board of Science Examiners. I must complete a certain number of hours of continuing education every two years. If I am arrested for a crime, or even if a client makes a complaint, I will be investigated and might lose my license.

Again, licensure alone doesn't eliminate all the bad apples, but it does cut out some. Further, when you choose a licensed therapist you know that if he or she is unethical in any way, they can be subjected to investigation and discipline. If you choose an unlicensed practitioner, you are not protected. We had one in Nevada County whom I reported to the Board after two women came to me for therapy, claiming he had sexually abused them in "therapy" sessions. Both were suicidal. The Board set up a sting operation and busted him for practicing without a license, but there was little they could do besides slap him on the wrist and tell him they'd watch him carefully. So he moved to Maine and set up shop there. Ain't this a great country, or what?

Anyone can hang out a shingle and say, "I do spiritual counseling" or "I'm a coach." They need have no education, have never passed an examination in the field, and have zero oversight. They can become famous, like Dr. Laura, whose doctorate is in physiology, not psychology.

I encourage you to make sure both your "therapist" and your "doctor" are legitimately licensed. In California you can go online at <gov. com> to check.

Okay, you've got a licensed person with an office where you can scream your head off if you wish. What next?

Check with people you trust who have had some experience of this therapist. If a therapist is any good, they have satisfied customers.

Finally, interview one or more prospective therapists. Some you can scratch off after a brief chat on the phone. For your final choice, be sure to have a face-to-face interview. Most good therapists welcome such an interview, because it's a two-way hire. I only work with people I feel good about and I want my clients to feel the same about me. So I always begin with a single session in which we get to know each other a bit and at the end of which we mutually decide whether we think this will be a good collaboration or not. You will probably have to pay for this interview but, believe me, it's well worth it. Find a therapist with whom you resonate positively. How do you feel inside your body when you are together? Trust your bodily wisdom.

Once you've decided to work with someone, please remember that you are the most important member of the team. It's you who will have to do the hard work, not your therapist. Be clear about what your goals in therapy are and don't hesitate to ask how what you are doing in your sessions will get you there. If something isn't working for you, say so. Keep giving your therapist feedback—if you have a complaint, raise it. Don't just swallow it or drop out. A good therapist will welcome your feedback and make it safe for you to offer it. Hopefully, your relationship will be a model of safety, clarity, and the open expression of feeling—the kind of relationship you deserve in your life from now on.

A SELECTED BIBLIOGRAPHY

Abrams, J., and Zweig, C., ed., *Meeting the Shadow: The Hidden Power of the Dark Side of Human Nature* (Los Angeles, 1991).

Bach, G., *The Intimate Enemy: How to Fight Fair in Love and Marriage* (New York, 1968).

Bader, E., and Pearson, P., *In Quest of the Mythical Mate: A Developmental Approach to Diagnosis and Treatment in Couples Therapy* (New York, 1988).

Barbach, L, *For Each Other: Sharing Sexual Intimacy* (New York, 1984).

Barbach, L., and Geisinger, D., *Going the Distance: Finding and Keeping Lifelong Love* (New York, 1993).

Bedier, J., *The Romance of Tristan and Iseult,* Belloc & Rosenfeld trans., (New York, 1965).

Bradshaw, J., *Creating Love: The Next Great Stage of Growth* (New York, 1992).

Campbell, S., *The Couple's Journey: Intimacy as a Path to Wholeness* (San Luis Obispo, 1980).

Cassell, C., *Swept Away: Why Women Fear Their Own Sexuality* (New York, 1984).

Chapman, G., *The Five Love Languages: How to Express Heartfelt Commitment to Your Mate* (Chicago, 2004).

De Rougement, D., *Love in the Western World* (New York, 1940).

Fisher, H., *Anatomy of Love: The Mysteries of Mating, Marriage, and Why We Stray* (New York, 1992).

Friday, Nancy, *My Secret Garden: Women's Sexual Fantasies* (1974).

Goleman, D., *Emotional Intelligence: Why It Can Matter More Than IQ* (New York, 1995).

Gordon, T., *Parent Effectiveness Training* (New York, 1970).

Gottman, J., and Silver, N., *The Seven Principles for Making Marriage Work* (London, 1999).

Gray, John, *What You Can Feel You Can Heal: A Guide for Enriching Relationships* (Mill Valley, 1984).
__________, *Men Are From Mars, Women Are From Venus: A Practical Guide for Improving Communication and Getting What You Want in Your Relationships* (New York, 1992).

Harley, W.F., Jr., *His Needs, Her Needs: Building an Affair-Proof Marriage* (Grand Rapids, Michigan, 2001).

Hendricks, G., and Hendricks, K., *Conscious Loving: The Journey to Co-Commitment* (New York, 1990).

Hendrix, H., *Getting the Love You Want: A Guide for Couples* (New York, 1988).
_________, *Keeping the Love You Find: A Guide for Singles* (New York, 1992).

Jampolsky, G., *Love Is Letting Go of Fear* (Millbrae, California, 1979).

Janov, A., *The Primal Scream* (New York, 1970).
________, *Imprints: The Lifelong Effects of the Birth Experience* (New York, 1983).

Johnson, B., *Fathers and Teachers: A Novel* (Charleston, 2008).
_________, *Snake Blossoms: Fabulations* (Berkeley, 1976).

Johnson, R., *We: Understanding the Psychology of Romantic Love* (San Francisco, 1983).

Keirsey, D., and Bates, M., *Please Understand Me: Character & Temperament Types* (Del Mar, 1978).

Kipnis, A., and Herron, E., *Gender War, Gender Peace: The Quest for Love and Justice between Men and Women* (New York, 1994).

Leboyer, F., *Birth Without Violence* (New York, 2009).

Lederer, W., and Jackson, D.D., *The Mirages of Marriage* (New York, 1968).

Lewis, C.S., *The Allegory of Love* (Oxford, 1971).

Lewis, T., Amini, F., and Lannon, R., *A General Theory of Love* (New York, 2000).

Lipton, B.H., and Bhaerman, S., *Spontaneous Evolution: Our Positive Future (And a Way to Get There from Here)* (Carlsbad, California, 2009).

Lowen, A., *Pleasure: A Creative Approach* (Baltimore, 1975).

Luthman, S., *Intimacy: The Essence of Male and Female* (San Rafael, 1972).

Miller, A., *Banished Knowledge: Facing Childhood Injuries* (New York, 1990).

Montague, Ashley, *Touching* (New York, 1971).

Moody, R.A., Jr., *Life After Life* (New York, 1975).

Moore, T., *Care of the Soul: A Guide for Cultivating Depth and Sacredness in Everyday Life* (New York, 1992).

________, *Soul Mates: Honoring the Mysteries of Love and Relationship* (New York, 1994).

Paul, J., and Paul, M., *Do I Have to Give Up Me to Be Loved by You?* (Minneapolis, 1983).

Peele, S., *Love and Addiction* (New York, 1975).

Perls, F., Hefferline, R.F., and Goodman, P., *Gestalt Therapy: Excitement and Growth in the Human Personality* (New York, 1951).

Pransky, G., *Divorce is Not the Answer: A Change of Heart Will Save Your Marriage* (Blue Ridge Summit, Pennsylvania, 1991).

Rogers, C., *Becoming Partners: Marriage and Its Alternatives* (New York, 1992).

Rosenberg, M.B., *Nonviolent Communication: A Language of Life* (Encinitas, California, 2003).

Rozak, T., *The Voice of the Earth* (New York, 1992).

Rubin, T.I., *The Angry Book* (New York, 1969).

Satir, V., *Peoplemaking* (Palo Alto, 1972).

Scarf, M., *Intimate Partners: Patterns in Love and Marriage* (New York, 1987).

Schaef, A.W., *Escape From Intimacy* (New York, 1989).

Shakespeare, W., *The Complete Plays and Poems*, ed. Neilson, W.A., and Hill, C.J., (Cambridge, 1942).

Siegel, D.J., *mindsight: The New Science of Personal Transformation* (New York, 2010).

Stettbacher, K., *Making Sense of Suffering: The Healing Confrontation with the Past* (New York, 1991).

Tannen, D., *That's Not What I Meant! How Conversational Style Makes or Breaks Relationships* (New York, 1986).

Tolle, E., *The Power of Now: A Guide to Spiritual Enlightenment* (Novato, California, 1999).

Verney, T., *The Secret Life of the Unborn Child* (New York, 1981).

Watzlawick, P., Beavin, J., and Jackson, D.D., *Pragmatics of Human Communication: A Study of Interactional Patterns, Pathologies, and Paradoxes* (New York, 1987).

Weinstein, M., and Goodman, J., *Playfair* (San Luis Obispo, 1980).

Welwood, J., *Journey of the Heart: Intimate Relationship and the Path of Love* (New York, 1990).

Whorf, B., *Language, Thought, and Reality* (Cambridge, 1956).

Zilbergeld, B., *Male Sexuality* (New York, 1978).

About the Author

Belden Johnson began his career as a mild-mannered college instructor in English and Creative Writing at the universities of Iowa and Maryland while also writing seven novels, one of which, *Fathers and Teachers*, is available on Amazon. He has also published a book of poems and stories entitled *Snake Blossoms*, which is currently a collector's item, that is to say, out of print.

In 1976 he began training as a marriage and family therapist with particular attention to family systems, the importance of feelings, and communications skills. He has a three year training in primal therapy, two years in bioenergetics, and a year of Gestalt therapy. His primary interest has been what happens within an individual inside of a relationship. In 1979 he co-founded The Primal Center in Berkeley, California, with Dr. Stephen Khamsi. He has published widely professionally on such topics as relationship, primal therapy, shamanism, fatherhood, and parenting.

He has been (mostly) happily married to Dr. Yashi Johnson for twenty-one years as of this writing. They have a blended family of four rather remarkable children. They are also partners at The Center for Inner Visions in Nevada City, California. They live in a little house in the big woods with a family of bears, several bobcats, two hawks, one eagle, and a dozen bluebirds as their nearest neighbors.

A lifelong athlete, Belden loves playing softball and basketball. He also backpacks, fishes, and hikes the High Sierra.

Belden would be honored to hear from you. You can contact him through The Center for Inner Visions website at <centerforinnervisions. com>.

Made in United States
Orlando, FL
02 May 2022

17421409R10153